THE
COMPETENCE
GAME
How to Find, Use,
and Keep
Competent Employees

RUTH W. STIDGER

Editorial Director
International Group
Technical Publishing Company
A Company of the Dun & Bradstreet Corporation

Illustrations by Arthur Arias

THE COMPETENCE GAME

How to Find, Use, and Keep Competent Employees

THOMOND PRESS
An Elsevier Professional Publication

Thomond Press is an Imprint of Elsevier North Holland, Inc.
52 Vanderbilt Avenue, New York, New York 10017

Distributed to the book trade in the United States
by Van Nostrand Reinhold Company
and in Canada by Van Nostrand Reinhold Ltd.

Library of Congress Cataloging in Publication Data

Stidger, Ruth W 1939–
    The competence game: how to find, use, and keep competent employees
    "An Elsevier professional publication."

    Includes index.
    1. Recruiting of employees. 2. Employees, Rating of. 3. Employee
    motivation. 4. Industrial relations. I. Title.
HF5549.5.R44S76   658.3′11   80-17657
ISBN 0-444-00453-X

Desk Editor John Haber
Design Edmée Froment
Art Editor Virginia Kudlak
Illustrations by Arthur Arias
Production Manager Joanne Jay
Compositor Publishers Phototype, Inc.
Printer Haddon Craftsmen

Manufactured in the United States of America

For Howe, who shares my belief
in the importance of competence.

CONTENTS

PREFACE

"We both believed . . . that the only sin on earth was to do things badly."

—Ayn Rand, *Atlas Shrugged*

This book will tell you how successful executives nationwide find, identify, and keep the most competent workers so that you can apply the same techniques to your own operation. The pages you are about to read will not be popular with those groups that support equal rewards for all without regard to the efforts used by an individual to earn his or her living. But the purpose of the book is not to please such groups; rather, I believe that these pages can help managers and executives who believe in and want competent work and workers.

Special thanks go to my research assistant, Susan Saylor, who used her psychological research training to help design the questionnaires for both executives and workers. Without her careful tabulation of results and interpretations of the statistics, this book could not have been completed. Thanks also to Lorraine Yegge, who checked the legality of or found validation for points that might be affected by rulings of the U.S. Equal Employment Opportunities Commission. And a sincere word of appreciation for Arthur A. Arias, whose cartoons help illustrate the importance of competence in successful business operation.

INTRODUCTION

Are there still competent workers? If so, how do you find and hire them for a salary you can afford? And, assuming you employ competent workers, how do you keep them from leaving your company? And, how do you define competence as it applies to your operations?

In the past two or three years, these questions have been raised repeatedly at professional meetings attended by both myself and fellow managers. These questions were always followed by heated discussions—sometimes accompanied by flaring tempers as managers railed against a seeming decreasing interest in hard work, an increase in government employment regulations, and higher inflation-forced salary levels.

I had the same problems as other managers. And, if you are a part of management, so do you.

Because I wanted to find answers to these problems, I began the research that led to the writing of *The Competence Game.*

WHAT IS A COMPETENT WORKER?

The dictionary will tell you that competence means having sufficient ability to do a job. But most managers want more than this when they seek a competent employee. My personal definition of a competent worker is one able to do a job well and willing to put in the effort required to complete a high volume of good-quality work. Before reading the rest of this book, you should determine your own definition of competence, preferably by writing it on a notepad so that you can refer to it as you read.

HARD WORK IS DECLINING

It's not just your imagination—or mine. U. S. Department of Labor statistics show that productivity is now *declining* at a rate of 4.5% a year. Productivity growth in the United States is now the lowest among all of the major Western industrialized nations, according to a recent report in the *Financial Times* of London.

Even on a long-term basis, U. S. productivity grew only about 30% between 1967 and 1978—certainly much lower than the inflation rate for the same period, and in fact probably a major cause of our high rate of inflation. During the same period, West Germany *increased* its productivity about 70%, and Japanese productivity grew more than 100%.

Causes for the decline of productivity in the United States are probably many. One small business owner blames it on the fact that work is completed in locations away from the home, which means that many younger workers have never seen anyone work and don't even know what hard work means.

The individual manager can also be directly responsible for this decline. Even good workers can be "turned off" if managers do not use their work wisely or well. Union leaders know this fact and in many cases use managerial bumbling to obtain and keep their positions.

"Soft" management—avoiding employee productivity and competence problems—is also often responsible for declining productivity. The manager who overlooks an employee's poor quality work is not doing anyone a favor. One executive interviewed summed up the problem well. "The uncorrected, inadequate worker left alone will simply remain that way," he said.

Can you, as an individual manager, overcome this decline in productivity and hard work? Yes. This book was planned and written to tell you how some of the top U. S. managers make the corrections necessary to halt productivity and competence problems.

HARD WORKERS EXIST

Much as managers complain about the difficulty of finding good workers, competent employees do exist. What makes hard workers put more effort into their jobs? A survey to identify work attitudes that typify the competent employee seemed an ideal way to pinpoint facts. Chapter 1 will give you the answers to what a competent worker is, as identified by survey results from 1,000 dual questionnaires.

Once you have read the results of this survey, you can look for the attitudes identified when you complete your own interviewing.

COMPETENCE: YOUR KEY TO MONEY AND ADVANCEMENT

If you want to make it to better positions in your own career, and if you want the bottom line of your operation to always look good, you *need* competence. You need competence in your employees, as well as your own competence. This book can help you find, use, and keep those hard workers—the ones who can ensure your own success.

GOVERNMENT REGULATIONS AND COMPETENCE

Certain hiring and personnel guidelines are necessary to comply with federal and state laws. Some managers believe that these laws are designed to protect the incompetent, but we do not agree. Some managers' fear of the laws and misunderstanding of their interpretation do, indeed, often protect the incompetent.

The laws, and various interpretations of them, are intended to provide adequate opportunities without regard to race, sex, or age of the applicant. Often, personnel and other managers overreact to these laws and hesitate to reject incompetent applicants. This book will help you determine legal ways to find, best use, and keep the most competent workers.

CHAPTER ONE

It is still legal to hire a competent person.

WHAT IS A COMPETENT EMPLOYEE?

All managers want employees who do their work well and at an affordable wage. Depending on the work to be done, the ability to be creative, to work alone, or to supervise others may also be needed. However, naming the qualities we want in employees does not ensure that we will find them.

What can the manager do when interviewing prospective employees to increase the chances of finding one who is competent? To multiply the chances, the author and a psychological researcher designed a survey that attempts to pinpoint the work attitudes and personality traits of employees who are considered most competent by their supervisors. Although survey results such as these can never provide *absolute* rules for competence characteristics, they can give the manager some general guidelines to keep in mind when interviewing.

SURVEY RESULTS

What makes top-rated employees, according to the results of the survey conducted?

Top-rated workers put family or love first in order of what's important to them.

TABLE 1. Employees Who Returned the Survey

Office workers	21.7%
Sales workers	13.0%
Factory/production workers	10.9%
Managerial workers	15.2%
Professional workers	19.5%
Service workers	19.7%

Top-rated workers take the most pride in their work.

Top-rated workers work long weeks.

Top-rated workers are least likely to have college degrees.

Top-rated workers think money is important, but not nearly as necessary as the satisfaction of doing a job well.

Top-rated workers think accuracy is the most important element of a job well done.

The questionnaires used were dual. The supervisor was asked to rate the competence level of five employees in a range from the best worker (to be rated #1) down to the one considered the least competent (to be rated #5). These rated employees were then given a work attitude questionnaire, coded so that we could match work attitudes with the level of competence rating given by their supervisors. In all cases, complete anonymity was assured to protect the jobs and futures of those who participated in the survey.

A total of 1,000 dual questionnaires were given to cooperating supervisors. Replies were further broken down by type of work involved—sales, office, industrial, service, managerial, professional, and so on (see Table 1).

To provide additional information, managers in 100 operations were interviewed in depth about the problems of finding and keeping competent employees and the solutions each had found.

ASK ABOUT WORK SPEED

When workers and supervisors rated work performance (see Table 2), top-rated (#1) employees were generally overly modest about their performance, while the lowest-rated (#5) workers weren't willing to admit low volume or poor quality. On work

TABLE 2. Work Performance as Related to Competence; Workers' and Supervisors' Views[a]

How work compares with that of co-workers, by area of work	#1 views		#2 views		#3 views		#4 views		#5 views	
	Worker	Supr.	Worker	Supr.	Worker	Supr.	Worker	Supr.	Worker	Supr.
Volume of work										
Worker does										
Less	—	—	—	18.2	—	—	13.4	28.6	23.7	71.4
Same	51.2	7.7	43.4	36.4	71.4	44.4	52.1	57.1	51.0	28.6
More	48.8	92.3	56.6	45.4	29.6	55.6	34.5	14.3	25.3	—
Speed of work										
Worker is										
Slower	7.1	—	—	27.3	14.3	11.1	55.9	42.9	26.2	85.7
Same	28.6	15.4	57.3	36.4	58.3	66.7	20.9	57.1	24.2	14.3
Faster	64.3	84.6	42.7	36.3	27.4	22.2	23.2	—	49.6	—
Quality of work										
Poorer	—	—	—	18.2	—	—	28.2	14.3	23.7	71.4
Same	21.4	15.0	54.8	36.4	28.6	68.3	34.2	85.7	25.9	28.6
Better	78.6	85.0	44.2	45.4	71.4	31.7	37.6	—	50.4	—

[a]In percent of respondents.

speed, employers and employees were in good agreement. Employees rated much as their bosses did on work speed, which might make this a good area to include in an interview. According to survey results, the employee's answer is most likely to agree later with your evaluation of the worker.

"I always ask about all three areas," said a department head in a large retail chain. "But job applicants are most likely to tell the truth about their work speed."

EMPLOYEE RANKING

"I always rank job applicants on a scale of 1–10, with 1 at the top," a district sales manager told us. "And at the end of each quarter, I rank each employee in the same way. Those who get a rating below 5 are given job counseling."

This kind of rating can be too subjective unless a list of performance standards is established. But we decided to see how managers would rank the workers we surveyed. As Table 3 shows, the average #1 employee rated a 1.8; the #5 employee averaged 6.9.

TABLE 3. How Supervisors Ranked All Five Levels of Employees on a Competence Scale of 1–10

Employee rating	#1	#2	#3	#4	#5
Competence rating	1.8	2.5	4.2	6.0	6.9

TABLE 4. What's Most Important to Employees, as Related to Competence[a]

	#1 goal	#2 goal	#3 goal	#4 goal	#5 goal
#1-rated worker:					
Family or love	83.7	7.7	—	—	8.6
Money	8.3	7.8	17.0	24.6	42.3
Work	8.0	53.8	30.3	6.5	—
Friends	—	15.4	29.7	30.4	25.9
Home	—	15.3	23.0	38.5	23.2
#2-rated worker:					
Family or love	77.4	1.0	3.6	—	18.0
Home	11.6	21.9	21.7	35.7	11.1
Money	11.0	9.8	21.3	20.6	37.3
Friends	—	56.2	19.2	10.9	11.7
Work	—	11.1	34.2	32.8	21.9
#3-rated worker:					
Family or love	73.5	16.9	—	—	9.6
Home	14.2	14.0	12.9	30.3	28.6
Money	12.3	11.4	37.6	24.7	14.0
Friends	—	28.6	31.3	16.7	23.4
Work	—	29.1	18.2	28.3	24.4
#4-rated worker:					
Family or love	54.0	11.9	17.4	—	16.7
Money	29.6	9.2	28.3	4.7	27.6
Friends	16.4	29.3	14.9	27.4	12.0
Home	—	32.9	24.5	17.0	25.6
Work	—	16.7	14.9	50.9	18.1
#5-rated worker:					
Family or love	41.3	8.8	23.2	9.0	17.7
Money	36.4	9.6	8.7	18.0	27.3
Home	22.3	10.2	10.9	45.0	11.6
Friends	—	57.1	14.3	12.9	15.7
Work	—	14.3	42.9	15.1	27.7

[a]In percent.

THEY DON'T WORK ONLY FOR MONEY

The most competent workers aren't as concerned about money as are less competent ones, according to survey results (see Table 4). Among those surveyed, competence levels went down as the percentage listing money as *most important* went up.

More important to the hiring manager is how important the worker considers his or her work. Most #1 employees rated it second most important after family and/or love. As competence ratings of workers surveyed went down, so did their opinion of work's importance in their own lives.

"It's hard to establish how important work is during a job interview," cautioned the head of a data processing unit. "I usually ask applicants to tell me what they like and don't like about work, and how work fits into their lifestyle."

LONG HOURS FOR TOP PERFORMERS

Do the longer hours worked by employees rated #1 and #2 make them appear more competent, or do competent workers put in more time? If the work gets done well, most managers won't care which answer is right.

Among those surveyed, top-rated performers definitely put in long work hours (see Table 5), while the lowest-rated (#5) workers kept at it 40 hours or less per week. The willingness to work long hours will probably be of most importance to managers hiring *salaried employees,* since such workers are generally paid a straight salary with no overtime, and the extra hours won't mean extra costs for the competence gained.

"I always ask applicants if they are willing to put in long hours when necessary," reported a magazine publisher. "Five o'clockers don't fit in well with a deadline-oriented business like ours."

TABLE 5. The Average Work Week as Related to Competence[a]

Hours/week	#1 worker	#2 worker	#3 worker	#4 worker	#5 worker
Over 50	25.3	—	—	—	—
41–50	28.6	32.8	27.6	—	—
35–40	42.9	56.2	58.1	82.8	51.7
Under 35	2.9	11.0	14.3	17.2	48.3

[a]In percent.

PINPOINTING IMPORTANT WORK TRAITS

Can you tell a competent employee by what he or she thinks is the most important aspect of work? You can test what survey respondents identified as important (see Table 6) to judge for yourself. Percentages include respondents who ranked a work element as first, second, or third most important in a list of 15 work elements.

TABLE 6. Work Elements Considered Most Important by Employees, as Related to Competence[a]

Work factor	#1 worker	#2 worker	#3 worker	#4 worker	#5 worker
Accuracy	61.9	44.6	56.0	51.2	12.4
Arriving on time	36.4	18.2	22.1	25.0	37.4
Completing work needed whether assigned or not	35.7	27.3	22.2	—	12.4
Getting along well with clients	35.6	52.6	11.1	—	1.25
Completing work assigned	21.3	—	22.2	24.9	24.3
Speed of work	20.7	19.5	—	13.4	—
Sticking to a job until completed	14.2	9.1	—	12.3	12.1
Getting along with co-workers	14.1	18.2	—	12.0	37.3
Improving company performance	14.0	—	11.0	—	11.9
Creativity	7.1	9.1	10.8	12.4	—
Learning new or improved work methods	7.0	9.0	11.1	12.2	12.3
Increasing own salary	6.8	18.2	22.2	—	25.1
Increasing company profits	6.7	9.0	21.8	—	12.1
Improving work performance	—	—	33.2	12.1	37.3
Improving own status or position within company	—	—	—	—	12.3

[a]Percent rating each factor (1, 2, or 3) in list of 15 factors.

Accuracy was the most important to many good workers, which may mean that accuracy should be given special weight in preemployment tests. For example, a typist who tests at 50 words per minute with one error might be preferable to one who tests at 80 words per minute with 16 errors, according to survey findings.

Interestingly, not many #5 workers rated accuracy as important. They were more concerned with getting to work on time, getting along with co-workers, and churning out assigned tasks.

Other patterns can be spotted in the survey results. For example, top performers believe it is more important to get along with customers or clients than with co-workers. These top-rated employees also believe that it's important to complete work that needs to be done whether that work is assigned to them or not. They put the importance of such tasks ahead of finalizing assigned work. The answers of #3s, #4s, and #5s do not follow the same pattern.

As competence ratings decreased, the importance workers gave to increasing their own salaries and status grew. Work speed was more important than money to the top performers.

PRIDE IN WORK EQUALS COMPETENCE

The worker who takes most pride in his or her work is likely to be the most competent, according to survey results (see Table 7). When asked how they feel about work, employees rated #1 said they take pride in it, like it, or consider it the most important fac-

TABLE 7. How Respondents Feel About Work[a]

	#1 worker	#2 worker	#3 worker	#4 worker	#5 worker
Take pride in work	52.5	41.5	27.0	25.8	—
Like work	25.3	20.8	8.1	27.3	40.8
Work is most important factor	22.2	9.6	—	—	—
Don't mind work	—	10.2	37.7	19.3	15.9
Have to do it	—	18.9	27.2	18.5	29.0
Dislike work very much	—	—	—	9.1	14.3

[a]In percent.

tor in their lives. As competence levels of ratings went down, so did pride in work and positive feelings about it. Workers rated #4 or #5 in the survey were more apt to have an active dislike of work.

"The question here is whether they dislike work because they're not competent, or whether they're not good because they're doing work they dislike," one office manager replied to an interview question. "The moral is the same—hire people who like what they will have to do."

HIRE SELF-MADE WORKERS

A college degree doesn't necessarily equal competence, according to survey results (see Table 8). Most #1-rated workers had no college degree, whereas about 40% of the #5-rated workers had a B.A. or higher degrees. The greatest percentage of workers with no more than an eighth grade education had #1 ratings.

"I hope this puts a stop to supervisors writing down 'college degree required' on job requisitions," quipped one corporate personnel manager. "They [the supervisors] think it's the thing to do, I guess."

GOOD WORKERS EXPECT MORE MONEY

Top performers expect more in the way of money and may view a salary as fair, while less competent workers look on the salary as very good, survey results show. With one employee at each level of competence from each company, the most competent workers were most likely to feel their salary was average or below

TABLE 8. Competence as Related to Education[a]

Highest level of education completed	#1 worker	#2 worker	#3 worker	#4 worker	#5 worker
Graduate degree	—	—	3.2	—	14.5
Bachelor's degree	13.4	30.3	59.8	42.8	25.6
Some college	27.9	48.7	12.2	14.3	24.1
High school	29.1	10.9	24.8	32.4	13.8
Grade school	28.6	10.1	—	10.5	22.0

[a]In percent.

TABLE 9. Does Payment or Worker Treatment Affect Competence?[a]

Worker's views	#1 worker	#2 worker	#3 worker	#4 worker	#5 worker
Company does not pay well	19.8	37.6	21.3	—	28.6
Company pays fairly	71.2	62.4	38.1	81.2	57.1
Company pays very well	10.0	—	40.6	18.8	14.3
Company is not usually fair	—	22.2	14.3	—	21.0
Company is usually fair	45.4	33.4	28.6	61.2	39.3
Company is very supportive of workers	54.6	44.3	57.1	38.8	39.7

[a]In percent.

average (see Table 9), even though they also rated money as not as important to them as the work itself.

"The best workers expect to be paid for their competence," said one office manager. "They don't harp on money all of the time, but if it isn't there, they'll leave sooner or later."

CHAPTER TWO

Recommend good job applicants to another firm if you don't have a job; then you'll know where to find them when you do.

SEARCHING FOR COMPETENT PEOPLE

When you have a job vacancy, where and how you search to fill it will largely determine how competent your applicants will be, according to interviews of managers surveyed. There are several basic ways to look for employees, these executives reported:

Recommendations from current employees.

Recommendations from persons in your industry.

State or federal government employment or job-training agencies.

Private employment or recruiting agencies.

Newspaper advertising.

Signs (for walk-in applications).

School referral services.

Intern programs.

Different types of jobs may require different types of recruiting, as is shown by survey results (see Table 10). Service workers and managerial employees were least likely to be recruited by newspaper advertisements, results showed. Personal referrals ranked high for all types of hiring.

TABLE 10. How Employers Find Workers[a]

Type of worker	Newspaper ads			Employment agencies			Personal references		
	Never	Sometimes	Always	Never	Sometimes	Always	Never	Sometimes	Always
Office workers	38.2	26.0	45.8	37.4	51.2	11.4	12.3	62.5	25.2
Service workers	52.1	11.9	36.0	37.2	37.8	24.9	12.7	51.1	36.2
Salespeople	33.2	31.6	35.2	51.0	32.3	16.7	—	52.6	47.4
Factory workers	30.8	32.7	36.5	76.4	23.6	—	19.7	40.3	40.0
Managerial workers	44.5	34.2	21.3	55.6	32.3	—	—	55.6	44.4
Professional workers	37.6	25.4	37.0	42.9	42.8	—	—	37.9	62.1

[a]Percent of time method is used.

WATCH THE PERSONNEL DEPARTMENT'S TOES

Some managers refuse to get involved with the initial search for competent workers; others take over the whole search, wasting their own time and making enemies in the personnel department. According to employers interviewed, the best results come from a middle-of-the-road approach.

"Our personnel people are bright," one sales executive said, "but they don't know our industry—they know interviewing techniques and how to do the payroll. I was getting tired of having to personally see every applicant they found. I decided it was time for a talk."

This executive asked the head of the personnel department for an interview to discover, in a nonhostile way, what the problems were. "I suggested sources of competent industry applicants, mandatory skills requirements to screen out the unqualified, and the work needs of our department. Then I got out of the way, and let the personnel department conduct the initial search for a competent worker."

Some types of recruiting do not lend themselves to much initial personnel department involvement—recruiting by means of personal recommendations, for example.

"Good personnel people won't resent your involvement here *if* you keep them informed so that they can meet legal requirements, such as notifying state employment offices of job openings first," the executive said.

GOVERNMENT AGENCIES: KNOW *YOUR* RIGHTS

State and federal employment and/or job-training agencies are often used to recruit workers because they charge neither employer nor employee. In some states, such as New York, employers are *required* to place a job order with the state agency before it is given to others. These facts do not mean that a government agency can supply you with competent applicants in every case, nor that you must hire from one. As government employment laws tighten, it is important to know *your* rights as an employer, as well as being aware of employment laws and regulations.

In working with a government or any other employment agency, executives interviewed recommend that you follow these basic steps:

1. Prepare a written job specification listing very precisely all skills and experience required of the applicant, as well as the exact duties the worker will perform if hired.
2. Insist that *only* qualified applicants be sent to you for an interview. You are *not* required to consider unqualified applicants, without necessary skills or education. If unqualified applicants are sent, inform the agency in writing that *only* qualified applicants will be interviewed—and then enforce this rule by refusing to start or continue an interview once an applicant is identified as being unqualified. This will save your time and that of unqualified applicants, although the agencies involved may then have a shorter list of daily interviews arranged.
3. Test applicants' skills, where these can be measured and are related to the job vacancy to be filled. Use the same test for *each* applicant for the job, and use the same test scoring system throughout. Typing, dictation, spelling, math, and editing are some of the types of tests that can be given. Scoring may be for speed and accuracy as related to work requirements.
4. Look at past work in lieu of a test where this is more appropriate. Writers, editors, artists, salespeople, and others should be able to provide samples of their work, whether this consists of a graphic portfolio or a sales presentation and sales record sheets. Compare the results of past performance with the job skills needed by your firm.

5. Let the agency know in advance that you *always* check work references, and then be sure to do so.
6. Ask the agency whether it has given any tests, and if so, ask to see the results of these.
7. Be aware of and obey federal and state laws that prohibit exclusion of applicants on the basis of sex, race, religion, age, and so on. Also be aware of the fact that you are *not required* to hire an applicant if he or she is not qualified.

PRIVATE AGENCIES—DOLLARS VERSUS BENEFITS

When using private employment agencies, the rules set out above will raise the competence level of the applicants sent to you, too. But if you hire the applicant, one of you—probably your company—will pay a fee. With fees ranging from 5 to 15% of the person's first-year salary, the applicants you get *should* be competent. This is not always the case, and there is a simple solution: Stop using any private agency that sends you more than one unqualified applicant and tell agency owners why you have stopped using their services.

Agencies are an expensive way to find competent workers, and should be avoided except in special cases, said the executives interviewed. What are the special cases that warrant use of private agencies? If you are looking for a very specialized skill, you may wish to use a recruiting agency. A good recruiting agency will check competent workers at competitive companies—something you might prefer not to do yourself.

Another reason to use private agencies is an urgent need for a competent person, when you can't wait for other methods to work. In this case, be sure to use an agency that specializes in your industry (there will almost surely be at least one of these in your city if you make an effort to find it). Follow the same steps as you do when working with a government agency, but expect and insist on a much more thorough screening of applicants before you receive them for an interview.

CALL THE RIGHT SCHOOL

School referral services can help you find competent workers— usually at no cost to you or to the applicant. One of the secrets, according to managers interviewed, is to call a school that both trains workers in the skills you need *and* has a competently run placement office. Without both features, you can waste a lot of time.

"We needed a layout artist that could read Chinese," a magazine publisher reported. "In our search we called two schools. One was a Chinese art school, and it seemed the most logical place to find our artist. Not so. The placement counselor sent us a girl with filing experience, even though we were explicit in requesting an experienced layout artist.

"We hired our artist through a local graphics training school, with a placement officer who sent us one applicant, too—but one who filled our specialized job needs."

You won't know which schools send competent applicants until you've tried them, of course. By following the same rules you use when dealing with employment agencies, however, you should be able to increase the ratio of competent applicants sent to you and to determine which schools to call for future vacancies.

INTERNS AREN'T FOREVER

The use of interns is a good and an inexpensive way to find competent workers, too: They provide a way to try an employee without hiring him or her. Contacting schools with intern programs aimed at your industry is the first step, supervisors say. If the school has a work/study or intern program, check these factors.

1. How are interns chosen? Are applicants screened before they are sent to you? A "yes" answer increases your chances of finding a competent employee. Do you have a choice of interns? Again, a "yes" is a good sign.
2. What kinds of work can you give interns? Be wary of programs that let you use the intern for just any kind of work. A good program and a good school will require that you provide work in the intern's area of specialty.
3. How near to graduation is the intern? For best results, the intern should be able to move directly from internship to graduation to your employment—if he or she works out—within a period of weeks or even days from the end of the internship.
4. How long is the internship? One semester is the minimum

most executives say they will consider. This is because the intern will need considerable training in your company's way of working. A full school year is a better internship period.

5. How much of the intern's time will you have? Four or five days per week are best; two days per week are the minimum, managers believe.
6. What will it cost? Some programs require that interns be paid minimum-wage rates; others suggest it, or merely hope you'll pay the intern's carfare and lunch bills.
7. What must you do? Good programs require progress reports from the intern's supervisor. The intern's grade will depend on these.

NEWSPAPER RECRUITING: MIXED RESULTS

Managers surveyed use newspapers' classified recruiting primarily for office, factory, and sales personnel (see Table 10). During interviews with managers, pro and con statements were made about the use of newspaper recruiting, and a number of guidelines emerged:

1. Don't use a blind ad. The most competent workers seldom respond to these, supervisors report.
2. Managerial, professional, and service workers are less likely to respond to any newspaper ad than are office, production, and sales workers.
3. Word the ad to screen out unqualified applicants, but be sure the wording meets Equal Employment Opportunities Commission requirements.
4. Choose the right newspaper. Every city has one paper that job applicants are most likely to read. In addition, use papers that go to the specialized work audiences you want to reach.
5. Don't scrimp on words to cut costs; the better results from a longer, more expressly worded ad will save money by saving interviewing time.
6. If you need an employee quickly, give a telephone number. Initial screening can be completed on the telephone and personal interview dates made quickly. Be sure the supervisor screening calls uses the same screening criteria for all applicants.

Planning the Ad. Planning can ensure that a newspaper advertisement will bring you more qualified applicants. Start with the job requisition, if you have one, and write a complete job description if you do not. Managers interviewed recommend that you make three lists: *work skills required, work experience required,* and *work attitudes required.*

Work skills required include proven selling ability for salespeople, the ability to operate specific machines for skilled factory workers, minimum typing and shorthand speeds for secretaries, and so on. Be sure to list *each* special skill needed, from the most to the least important.

Work experience and education required should be put into list format, too. If you are willing to do only minimal training, you may want to specify two years of experience in the field, for example. If you want someone who can supervise other workers, you may require five years' work experience and two years' supervisory experience in the same field. Educational needs should be related to job requirements.

Work attitudes to be listed should include those you expect in all of your employees. You may wish to include those that ranked high in competent employees surveyed (see Table 6), such as accuracy, work punctuality, and so on. Measurement of work attitudes in applicants is a subjective matter, and it is probably not legal to require specific work attitudes. It is legal, however, to request and expect certain attitudes in applicants and workers—assuming that you tell employees what standards have been set. It is also legal to dismiss workers who do not meet standards that are known, such as attendance standards.

Writing the Advertisement. Once your three lists are completed (see Figure 1), you will have the raw material you need to write an advertisement. The words in the lists are what you will use.

Begin with the shortest possible description of the job. In the example of Figure 1, "Secretary" would be such a short description. The manager providing these lists wrote the following ad:

Secretary: Accurate, dependable self-starter who can type 60+ wpm. Norelco dictaphone and 20-unit switchboard experience a must. Secretarial school, 1+ years experience a plus. Good salary and advancement possibilities. Phone 289-3434, Kay Smith, XYZ Company.

"I put the main points on the lists in the advertisement first," the manager reported. "Then I told applicants what I had to offer them. Our benefits aren't the greatest, so I didn't mention those."

Telling applicants what you will offer them (interesting work, a good salary, and so on) is essential to attracting competent applicants, managers report. Stressing skills, education, experience, and attitudes required will help weed out poor applicants who will only waste your interviewing time.

To provide examples in other fields, we asked managers to make lists for all work areas (see Table 11). In writing ads using these lists, or your own lists, simply include the elements shown, and add what you can offer the applicant. For example, an ad-

FIGURE 1. Typical lists used by managers to plan newspaper advertising for competent employees.

Job Title: Secretary

Work Skills:

Typing: 60 + wpm on IBM Selectric.

Dictation: Able to use Norelco dictaphone or equivalent.

Phone answering: Able to handle 20-unit switchboard, to take messages politely and accurately.

Work Experience and Education:

Secretarial school or equivalent training; 1+ year work experience.

Work Attitudes:

Accurate in work.

Dependable in attendance.

Able to work on own when boss is out of town.

TABLE 11. Typical Lists Used to Prepare Newspaper "Help Wanted" Ads for Several Types of Jobs

Job	Work skills	Experience/education	Attitudes
Typist	Type 50+ wpm on IBM Selectric, sort mail accurately, use Xerox.	High school graduate, no experience needed.	Accurate, dependable, willing to learn.
Hairdresser	Color work, cutting, shampoos and/or blowouts, permanents	Beautician's license with short courses in specialty areas, 2 years work experience and some clientele following.	Dependable, able to please clients.
Construction worker	Operate 3.5-yd^3 hydraulic shovel.	1+ years experience on shovel.	Dependable, fast, willing to work overtime.
Sales clerk	Math ability, sales personality, knowledge of electronic equipment.	High school grad, 1+ years selling experience.	Accurate, dependable, able to please customers.
Psychologist	R.E.T. abilities	M.A. a plus, R.E.T. training a must, 1+ years experience a plus.	Dependable, objective, able to empathize with patients.
Personnel manager	Interviewing, testing, supervising other interviewers.	Some college a plus; knowledge of interviewing, testing, legal factors; 10 years experience in field, 2+ years supervisory experience.	Able to complete needed work, dependable, compatible with coworkers.

vertisement written to attract a competent construction worker, using the lists given in Table 11, might read as follows:

Construction worker: Skilled, hydraulic shovel operator needed to run 3.5-cubic yard Brand X machine. Must be experienced, fast, dependable, and willing to work overtime as required. Top salary plus a chance at supervisor's spot in 6 months. Call 928-0339 from 8 to 11 A.M. S & N Construction.

When writing advertisements for service employees (such as waiters) or for sales clerks, it is important to stress customer-worker relationships. Payment should usually depend at least in part on sales made or services given, or the most competent applicants will look for jobs where such payments are provided.

A good example of the importance of immediate incentive payments is the case of a department store in a small Midwestern city. Before 1960, the store paid clerks a salary that met local standards, plus a very small commission depending on the average price of the merchandise sold in individual departments. For example, in the shoe department, commissions were 0.5%, and average sales per clerk in the department were $1,400 per week, which earned a commission of $7.00. However, the best salesman in the department regularly sold about $3,500 worth of shoes per week, adding $17.50 to his wage of $100 per week. His earnings were greater because he was courteous and was genuinely concerned about helping the customer find the best combination of the right style, size, and price in shoes. This meant repeat business.

In 1960, the store decided to dispense with cash incentives and offer profit sharing on a yearly basis that would approximately equal the value of the old plan. "Our top three people in the shoe department quit the first year," the store's manager reported. "Maybe we didn't present the new plan in a positive way. They went to stores that offered commissions, and our department's sales went down 11% that first year."

If you can offer incentives to the service worker, be sure to include this information in your advertising. For example, when writing an ad for the hairdresser mentioned in Table 11, your copy might read as follows:

Hairdresser: Customer-oriented, dependable licensed hairdresser with 2+ years of color, cutting, perm, and shampoo/blow-dry experience. Specialty certificates and clientele following a plus. Guaranteed wage with 40% of tabs plus tips. Apply in person, 9–11 A.M., Smith's Beauty Salon, 123 6th Avenue.

When writing ads to obtain competent professional workers, be precise about the skills needed. For example, an ad for the psychologist mentioned in Table 11 might read

Psychologist: Dependable, objective M.A., thoroughly trained in R.E.T. Workshops or internship at Rational Institute a plus. Work requires empathetic counselor for women's outpatient clinic. Send resumé detailing training and experience, including names of instructors and supervisors, as well as professional references, to the AB Clinic, 17 8th Avenue, New York, NY 10011.

When writing advertisements for management employees, be precise about skills and work attitudes needed. An ad for the personnel manager mentioned in Table 11 might read

Personnel manager: Experienced supervisor with 10+ years in personnel, 2+ years management experience. Extensive knowledge of legal, interviewing, testing aspects needed, plus ability to complete heavy recordkeeping workload on time. Must be able to motivate subordinates and work with managers hiring company personnel. College records and references will be checked thoroughly. Top salary plus good profit sharing. Send resumés to Controller, XYZ Company, 123 6th Avenue, New York City, NY 10011.

EMPLOYEE RECOMMENDATIONS: PROS AND CONS

Recruiting by asking employees to recommend applicants can be worthwhile if the employee is competent, and if he or she can judge competence in others. Managers interviewed reported that employees generally recommend friends remarkably like themselves.

"I had a bright secretary who recommended a friend for a clerk's position," one manager said. "She was fairly new at the time and I didn't yet realize how much of the day she spent on personal phone calls, how often she came in late, and so on. Her friend was bright, too, and a hard, competent worker—when he was around. He came in at 10:00, 11:00, whenever the mood hit." Both employees were eventually dismissed for continual tardiness.

"The real capper," this manager added, "is that the secretary got a job in London three months later by telling a business acquaintance she'd worked for me and by implying I would recommend her. He didn't check with me—just hired her."

On the other side of the coin, an employee *known* to be competent and dependable will usually recommend only good workers. He or she knows that poor quality performance by the applicant will reflect on his or her own judgment.

Most companies now offer a referral bonus to employees below management level. In smaller firms, this bonus may be as little as $25, while bonuses may be as much as $500 or more.

A rule of thumb used by one Midwestern retail chain to determine the amount of the referral bonus is to give a bonus equivalent to about 1% of the new employee's first year's salary. Thus the bonus for a sales clerk is $100, while bonuses for applicants referred for managerial positions are about $300.

An Eastern service association pays bonuses based on a percentage of the employment agency fee saved, currently 30% of the fee. This means that office worker referrals are worth about $150 to the employee making the recommendation.

WORD-OF-MOUTH RECRUITING—BY INDUSTRY

Referrals of applicants by people within the industry are a top source of competent employees if *you* can measure the competence of the person making the referral, said managers interviewed. It is also necessary to let your contacts know you have an opening. This means making some phone calls and mentioning your need at business lunches, cocktail parties, and so on.

Chances of finding competent employees by word-of-mouth referrals are increased if you are active in industry organizations and have regular contact with people who can provide possibly good applicants.

"Association listings of job applicants can be good or bad," one manager warned, looking at another source of in-industry referrals. "You can be sure such a list will include incompetent workers who've been unable to find work any other way, as well as competent workers. A key to separating the two types of applicants is to check job history. Those without bona fide jobs for a long period of time should have a valid reason, for example. If they don't, consider that a warning flag."

A variation on word-of-mouth recruiting is what one publisher interviewed called the "put them in a safe place" technique. "Whenever I see a competent salesperson," he said, "and I have no openings, I help him or her find a job with another company. Then, when I do have an opening, I call to see if he or she is still interested in working for me."

STREET-WISE RECRUITING

The least expensive form of recruiting involves simply placing a sign in the window. This method is most often used in small retail operations seeking sales clerks, or by service operations wanting service employees.

Chances of finding competent workers with this method of recruiting are improved, according to small business owners interviewed, by placing the sign inside the store or operation, rather than in the window.

"If the sign is near the cash register," reports a health food store owner, "and a customer inquires, you know that he or she at least has some knowledge of and interest in your products."

Wording, as in newspaper advertisement preparation, is the only other way to improve the quality of applicants inquiring about a vacancy advertised with in-store signs. Use the same listing method as recommended for preparation of newspaper ads, and be sure the sign spells out all the skills and qualities needed for the vacancy to be filled.

Word-of-mouth recruiting comes into play with signs, too, as a customer may mentally match the skills needed for the job with those of a friend or relative looking for work and tell that person about the vacancy.

CHAPTER THREE

EVALUATING THE APPLICATION

Application forms can be wonderful tools in finding competent employees, or they can actually hinder your task. The end result often depends on their design.

Before reading more, find a blank application form used by your company and examine it. Even if you cannot alter a poorly designed form, it is important to know the weak points so that you can work around them. If the form's design is poor and it *can* be redesigned, do so as quickly as possible. As you complete the redesign, however, be sure that the questions used are legal and that they do not violate Equal Employment Opportunities Commission rulings.

APPLICATION DESIGN: WHAT IT SHOULD INCLUDE

Contact information is the first kind of data needed on an employment application form. Be sure that this section requires the applicant's full name, address, social security number, home telephone number, work address, work telephone number, and a space to note whether or not the applicant can be discreetly called at work (see Figure 2). Do *not* ask for age, sex, race, re-

APPLICATION FOR EMPLOYMENT

Name: _____

Home address (number, street, city, state): _____

_____

Home phone: _____

Work: Company name _____

　　　　Company address _____

Work phone: _____

May we contact you at work, if your application is discussed only with you?

_____Yes _____No

FIGURE 2. Good opening section for an employment application form.

ligion, marital status, or other information that you cannot legally obtain.

Avoid meaningless or subjective questions such as condition of health, and depend on required preemployment physical examinations if health is a problem for insurance or other reasons. Applicants will probably check the answer that they believe you want to see or hear in regard to health, since they cannot accurately and objectively judge their state of health, anyway.

Employment history is your greatest competence screening tool, say the managers interviewed. This should come next on the application form. Applicants should complete this section, giving information about their most recent job first, and working progressively back through at least their last four jobs. According to managers surveyed, the most useful information (see Figure 3) includes the following:

Beginning and ending dates of the job—these should tally with ex-employers' records.

EMPLOYMENT HISTORY

Start with most recent job

Dates	Company name, address	Beginning salary	Immediate Supervisor	Summarize skills used, responsibilities
Began				
Left		Last salary	Company phone number	

Dates	Company name, address	Beginning salary	Immediate Supervisor	Summarize skills used, responsibilities
Began				
Left		Last salary	Company phone number	

Dates	Company name, address	Beginning salary	Immediate Supervisor	Summarize skills used, responsibilities
Began				
Left		Last salary	Company phone number	

Dates	Company name, address	Beginning salary	Immediate Supervisor	Summarize skills used, responsibilities
Began				
Left		Last salary	Company phone number	

FIGURE 3. Employment history section for an application form.

Company name, address, and phone number of ex-employers. If the applicant has the phone number, it will save you time when checking references.

Immediate supervisor's name—this is used when checking references, even though the supervisor may not be contacted directly (see Chapter 5).

Summary of job skills and responsibilities.

Salary when beginning and leaving the job.

Avoid meaningless or subjective questions, such as the reason for leaving a job. Most applicants reply with answers they think you want to hear, rather than the real reasons, said the managers we interviewed.

Ask about special skills or knowledge that suit the applicant to your industry. The most competent employees often have skills or non-job-related background that prepared them for their work, according to more than half of the executives interviewed. Careful wording of such a question or questions on the job application form can help you find competent employees more quickly (see Figure 4).

FIGURE 4. Ask the applicant to describe the position desired and the skills he or she has, since this can help you evaluate probable competence.

Position wanted:_____

Describe the job skills, background, or training that might help you complete the

job tasks for the position listed above. _____

_____

_____

_____

_____

_____

Briefly state your job goals. _____

_____

_____

_____

_____

FIGURE 5. Ask the applicant to state his or her job goals to help measure probable competence.

Ask about job goals as an additional way to measure work attitudes, aspirations, and so on (see Figure 5). Watch for attitudes that ranked high among competent employees surveyed.

Educational information should come next. If the personnel department plans to check with the various schools, there may be some point in using a lengthy section here. Managers interviewed often stated that virtually no educational checking is done within their hiring procedure. In this case, a simple question about educational levels reached is sufficient (see Figure 6).

Even though you may not have time to check educational background information, it is possible to roughly evaluate applicants with college degrees by checking the school's entrance requirements. "I recently hired a top-notch person with a degree from McGill," one executive reported during our interview. "She told me that the degree hadn't helped her because few U. S. man-

FIGURE 6. Lengthy educational information sections are unnecessary on applications, unless someone will actually check on the accuracy of the information given.

State highest level of education, last school attended, and grade point average.

_____

_____

_____

TABLE 12. Some Schools by Competitiveness of
Entrance Requirements[a]

School	Rating
Abilene Christian University (Texas)	A
Adelphi University (New York)	A
Allegheny College (Pennsylvania)	AA
American University (Washington, D.C.)	A
Amherst College (Massachusetts)	AAAA
Andrews University (Michigan)	A
Appalachian State University (North Carolina)	A
Arizona State University (Arizona)	A
Auburn University (Alabama)	A
Augusta College (Georgia)	A
Augustana College (Illinois)	A
Baldwin–Wallace College (Ohio)	A
Baylor University (Texas)	A
Bemidji State University (Minnesota)	A
Bennington College (Vermont)	AAA
Bentley College (Massachusetts)	A
Bethel College (Minnesota)	A
Biola College (California)	A
Biscayne College (Florida)	A
Bloomsburg State College (Pennsylvania)	A
Boston College (Massachusetts)	AA
Boston State College (Massachusetts)	AA
Boston University (Massachusetts)	AA
Bowdoin College (Maine)	AAAA
Bowling Green State University (Ohio)	A
Bradley University (Illinois)	A
Brandeis University (Massachusetts)	AAA
Bridgewater State College (Massachusetts)	A
Brigham Young University (Utah)	A
Brown University (Massachusetts)	AAAA
Bryant College (Rhode Island)	A
Bryn Mawr College (Pennsylvania)	AAAA
Bucknell University (Pennsylvania)	AAA
Butler University (Indiana)	A
California Institute of Technology	AAAA
California State (California)	A
Calvin College (Michigan)	A
Campbell College (North Carolina)	A
Canisius College (New York)	A
Carleton College (Minnesota)	AAA
Carnegie-Mellon University (Pennsylvania)	AAA
Case Western Reserve University (Ohio)	AAAA
Catholic University of America (Washington, D.C.)	A
Central Connecticut State College (Connecticut)	A
Central Missouri State University (Missouri)	A

[a]Schools not requesting admissions information in the format above are not included.

(*continued*)

TABLE 12 *(continued)*

School	Rating
Central Washington University (Washington)	A
The Claremont Colleges (California)	AAAA
Clarkson College of Technology (New York)	AA
Clarion State College (Pennsylvania)	A
Clark University (Massachusetts)	AA
Clemson University (South Carolina)	A
Cleveland State University (Ohio)	A
Colby College (Maine)	AAA
Colgate University (New York)	AAA
College of Charleston (South Carolina)	A
College of Holy Cross (Massachusetts)	AA
College of St. Catherine (Minnesota)	AA
College of the Sacred Heart (Puerto Rico)	A
College of William and Mary (Virginia)	AAA
Colorado College (Colorado)	AAA
Colorado State University (Colorado)	A
Columbia University (New York)	AAAA
Concordia College (Minnesota)	A
Cooper Union (New York)	AAAA
Cornell University (New York)	AAAA
Creighton University (Nebraska)	AA
Dartmouth College (New Hampshire)	AAAA
David Lipscomb College (Tennessee)	A
Davidson College (North Carolina)	AAA
Delta State College (Mississippi)	A
De Pauw University (Indiana)	AA
Denison University (Ohio)	A
DePaul University (Illinois)	AA
Drake University (Iowa)	A
Drexel University (Pennsylvania)	AA
Duke University (North Carolina)	AAA
Duquesne University (Pennsylvania)	A
East Carolina University (North Carolina)	A
East Stroudsburg State College (Pennsylvania)	A
Eastern Connecticut State College (Connecticut)	A
Eastern Illinois University (Illinois)	A
Edinboro State College (Pennsylvania)	A
Embry-Riddle Aeronautical University (Florida)	A
Emory University (Georgia)	AA
Fairfield University (Connecticut)	AA
Fairleigh Dickinson University (New Jersey)	A
Fashion Institute of Technology (New York)	A
Fitchburg State College (Massachusetts)	A
Flagler College (Florida)	A
Florida State University (Florida)	A
Florida Technological University (Florida)	A

(continued)

TABLE 12. Some Schools by Competitiveness of
Entrance Requirements[a] (*continued*)

School	Rating
Fordham University (New York)	AA
Framingham State College (Massachusetts)	A
Frostburg State College (Maryland)	A
Furman University (South Carolina)	A
Gannon College (Pennsylvania)	A
General Motors Institute (Michigan)	AAA
George Mason University (Virginia)	A
Georgetown University (Washington, D.C.)	AAA
Georgia College (Georgia)	A
Georgia Institute of Technology (Georgia)	A
Georgia State University (Georgia)	A
George Washington University (Washington, D.C.)	AA
Gonzaga University (Washington)	A
Grand Valley State College (Michigan)	A
Grinnell College (Iowa)	AAA
Grove City College (Pennsylvania)	A
Gustavus Adolphus College (Minnesota)	AA
Hamilton College (New York)	AAA
Harding College (Arizona)	A
Harvard University (Massachusetts)	AAAA
Haverford College (Pennsylvania)	AAAA
Hofstra University (New York)	A
Hope College (Michigan)	A
Howard University (Washington, D.C.)	A
Humboldt State University (California)	A
Illinois State University (Illinois)	A
Indiana University (Indiana)	A
Iona College (New York)	A
Iowa State University (Iowa)	AA
Ithaca College (New York)	A
Jacksonville University (Florida)	A
James Madison University (Virginia)	A
Jersey City State College (New Jersey)	A
John Carroll University (Ohio)	A
Johns Hopkins University (Maryland)	AAAA
Kalamazoo College (Michigan)	AAA
Kean College (New Jersey)	A
Kearney State College (Nebraska)	A
Kenyon College (Ohio)	AAA
Kutztown State College (Pennsylvania)	A
Lafayette College (Pennsylvania)	AAA
Lake Superior State College (Michigan)	A
La Salle College (Pennsylvania)	A
Lehigh University (Pennsylvania)	AAA
Lock Haven State College (Pennsylvania)	A
Loma Linda University (California)	A

(*continued*)

TABLE 12 *(continued)*

School	Rating
Long Island University (New York)	A
Longwood College (Virginia)	A
Louisiana State University (Louisiana)	A
Loyola University (Illinois)	A
Loyola University (Louisiana)	A
Manhattan College (New York)	A
Mansfield State College (Pennsylvania)	A
Marquette University (Wisconsin)	A
Mary Washington College (Virginia)	A
Marywood College (Pennsylvania)	A
Massachusetts Institute of Technology (Massachusetts)	AAAA
McGill University (Canada)	AA
Mercer University (Georgia)	A
Merrimack College (Massachusetts)	A
Miami University (Ohio)	A
Michigan State University (Michigan)	A
Michigan Technological University (Michigan)	A
Middlebury College (Vermont)	AAA
Midwestern State University (Texas)	A
Millersville State College (Pennsylvania)	A
Mississippi State University (Mississippi)	A
Mississippi University for Women (Mississippi)	A
Montclair State College (New Jersey)	A
Moorhead State University (Minnesota)	A
Mount Holyoke College (Massachusetts)	AAAA
New York University (New York)	AA
Niagara University (New York)	A
North Adams State College (Massachusetts)	A
North Texas State University (Texas)	A
Northeastern University (Massachusetts)	A
Northwestern University (Illinois)	AAA
Northern Arizona University (Arizona)	A
Northern Illinois University (Illinois)	A
Oakland University (Michigan)	A
Oberlin College (Ohio)	AAA
Ohio Northern University (Ohio)	A
Ohio Wesleyan University (Ohio)	A
Oklahoma State University (Oklahoma)	A
Old Dominion University (Virginia)	A
Oral Roberts University (Oklahoma)	A
Oregon College of Education (Oregon)	A
Oregon Institute of Technology (Oregon)	A
Oregon State University (Oregon)	A
Pace University (New York)	A
Pacific Lutheran University (Washington)	A
Pennsylvania State University (Pennsylvania)	A

(continued)

TABLE 12. Some Schools by Competitiveness of
Entrance Requirements*a* (*continued*)

School	Rating
Pepperdine University (California)	A
Polytechnic Institute of New York (New York)	AAA
Portland State University (Oregon)	A
Pratt Institute (New York)	A
Princeton University (New Jersey)	AAAA
Providence College (Rhode Island)	A
Purdue University (Indiana)	A
Quinnipiac College (Connecticut)	A
Radcliffe College (Massachusetts)	AAAA
Radford College (Vermont)	A
Ramapo College (New Jersey)	A
Reed College (Oregon)	AAA
Rhode Island College (Rhode Island)	A
Rice University (Texas)	AAAA
Rider College (New Jersey)	A
Rochester Institute of Technology (New York)	A
Roosevelt University (Illinois)	A
Rutgers University (New Jersey)	AA
St. Bonaventure University (New York)	A
St. John's University (New York)	A
St. Joseph's College (Pennsylvania)	AA
St. Lawrence University (New York)	AA
St. Louis University (Missouri)	A
St. Olaf College (Minnesota)	AA
St. Peter's College (New Jersey)	A
Salem State College (Massachusetts)	A
Salisbury State College (Maryland)	A
Samford University (Alabama)	A
Sam Houston State University (Texas)	A
San Diego State University (California)	A
San Francisco State University (California)	A
San Jose State University (California)	A
Seattle Pacific University (Washington)	A
Seattle University (Washington)	A
Seton Hall (New Jersey)	A
Shepherd College (West Virginia)	A
Shippenburg State College (Pennsylvania)	A
Siena College (New York)	A
Skidmore College (New York)	AA
Smith College (Massachusetts)	AAAA
Sonoma State College (California)	A
South Dakota State University (South Dakota)	A
Southeastern Massachusetts University (Massachusetts)	A
Southeastern Connecticut State College (Connecticut)	A
Southern Methodist University (Texas)	A
Springfield College (Massachusetts)	A

(*continued*)

TABLE 12 *(continued)*

School	Rating
Stanford University (California)	AAAA
State University of New York (New York)	AA
Stephen F. Austin State University (Texas)	A
Stetson University (Florida)	A
Stevens Institute of Technology (New Jersey)	AAA
Stockton State College (New Jersey)	A
Suffolk University (Massachusetts)	A
Swarthmore College (Pennsylvania)	AAAA
Syracuse University (New York)	A
Temple University (Pennsylvania)	A
Texas A & M University (Texas)	A
Texas Christian University (Texas)	A
Texas Technical University (Texas)	A
Towson State University (Maryland)	A
Trenton State College (New Jersey)	A
Trinity College (Connecticut)	AAA
Trinity University (Texas)	A
Tufts University (Massachusetts)	AAA
Tulane University (Louisiana)	AA
University of Akron (Ohio)	AA
University of Alabama (Alabama)	A
University of Arkansas (Arkansas)	A
University of Arizona (Arizona)	A
University of Bridgeport (Connecticut)	A
University of California (California)	AA
University of California (Berkeley Branch)	AAA
University of Chicago (Illinois)	AAA
University of Cincinnati (Ohio)	A
University of Colorado (Colorado)	A
University of Connecticut (Connecticut)	AA
University of Dayton (Ohio)	A
University of Delaware (Delaware)	A
University of Denver (Colorado)	A
University of Detroit (Michigan)	A
University of Evansville (Indiana)	A
University of Florida (Florida)	A
University of Georgia (Georgia)	A
University of Hartford (Connecticut)	A
University of Hawaii (Hawaii)	A
University of Houston (Texas)	A
University of Idaho (Idaho)	A
University of Illinois (Illinois)	AA
University of Iowa (Iowa)	A
University of Kentucky (Kentucky)	A
University of Louisville (Kentucky)	A
University of Lowell (Massachusetts)	A

(continued)

TABLE 12. Some Schools by Competitiveness of
Entrance Requirements[a] (*continued*)

School	Rating
University of Maine (Maine)	A
University of Maryland (Maryland)	A
University of Massachusetts (Massachusetts)	A
University of Miami (Florida)	A
University of Michigan (Michigan)	AA
University of Minnesota (Minnesota)	A
University of Mississippi (Mississippi)	A
University of Missouri (Missouri)	AA
University of Motevallo (Alabama)	A
University of New Hampshire (New Hampshire)	A
University of North Carolina (North Carolina)	AA
University of North Dakota (North Dakota)	A
University of Northern Colorado (Colorado)	A
University of Northern Iowa (Iowa)	A
University of Notre Dame (Illinois)	AAA
University of the Pacific (California)	A
University of Pennsylvania (Pennsylvania)	AAAA
University of Pittsburgh (Pennsylvania)	A
University of Portland (Oregon)	A
University of Puget Sound (Washington)	A
University of Rochester (New York)	AAA
University of Rhode Island (Rhode Island)	A
University of Richmond (Virginia)	A
University of San Francisco (California)	A
University of Santa Clara (California)	A
University of Scranton (Pennsylvania)	A
University of South Alabama (Alabama)	A
University of South Carolina (South Carolina)	A
University of South Dakota (South Dakota)	A
University of Southern California (California)	A
University of South Florida (Florida)	A
University of Tennessee (Tennessee)	A
University of Texas (Texas)	A
University of Tulsa (Oklahoma)	A
University of Utah (Utah)	A
University of Vermont (Vermont)	AA
University of Virginia (Virginia)	AAA
University of Washington (Washington)	AA
University of Wisconsin (Winconsin)	A
Utah State University (Utah)	A
Valdosta State College (Georgia)	A
Valparaiso University (Indiana)	A
Vassar College (New York)	AAA
Villanova University (Pennsylvania)	A
Virginia Commonwealth University (Vermont)	A
Wagner College (New York)	A

(*continued*)

TABLE 12 (*continued*)

School	Rating
Wake Forest University (North Carolina)	AA
Washington State University (Washington)	A
Washington University (Missouri)	AA
Wayne State University (Michigan)	A
Wellesley College (Massachusetts)	AAAA
Wesleyan University (Connecticut)	AAAA
West Chester State College (Pennsylvania)	A
Western Connecticut State College (Connecticut)	A
Western Illinois University (Illinois)	A
Western Michigan University (Michigan)	A
Western Washington University (Washington)	A
Westfield State College (Massachusetts)	A
Westminster College (Utah)	A
West Virginia University (West Virginia)	A
Widener College (Pennsylvania)	A
William Patterson College (New Jersey)	A
Williams College (Massachusetts)	AAAA
Winona State University (Minnesota)	A
Wittenberg University (Ohio)	A
Xavier University (Ohio)	A
Yale University (Connecticut)	AAAA
Youngstown State University (Ohio)	A

agers had even heard of her school. My reaction was, 'My God, it's tough to get into McGill.' So their loss was my gain."

Table 12 provides a list of schools that have high entrance standards. Whereas meeting competitive entrance requirements does not ensure that an applicant will be competent, it provides a quick way to measure the intelligence and performance levels required to enter the school from which the applicant has graduated.

Those with an AAAA rating are the most competitive, requiring the student to rank in the top 10–20% of his or her class, to have a grade average of B+ or better, to have a median SAT score of 625–800, and to score 28 or above on the ACT test.

Schools marked AAA have highly competitive entrance requirements. These include a B or better grade average, a ranking in the top 20–30% of the class, a score of 575–625 on the SAT, and a score of 26–28 on the ACT.

Schools with an AA rating have very competitive entrance requirements. These include carrying a B− or better grade average, ranking in the top 30–50% of the class, scoring 525 or better on the SAT, and scoring 23 or more on the ACT.

Schools with an A rating have competitive entrance requirements. These include carrying a C or better grade average, ranking in the top two thirds of the class, and having SAT scores over 500 and an ACT score over 22.

The source of applicant referral should be noted on the application form so that referral fees or employee bonuses can be paid when applicable, and so that you can later check the sources of your most competent workers.

Other questions may be added to the application form as needed for individual operations. For example, if the employee must be bonded, it is necessary to check whether he or she is bondable.

EXAMINING AN APPLICATION FORM

To help in critically examining your own application form and to learn which areas you may need to change (or avoid, if they can't be changed), we obtained a typical employment application form from one of the country's largest firms (see Figure 7). A line-by-line examination of this form can help in checking your own application for strengths and weaknesses.

The name, address, and phone number section is rather standard. However, no room is given for a business address or phone number. The date of application and social security number are requested at the beginning of the form to make recordkeeping easier for the personnel department.

Age questions included in this sample employment application form are those currently allowed by law. Some firms omit this question, since it will be obvious from the educational history whether an applicant is 18, and since the work history provides the best guidelines to age. The question is considered a meaningless one by many firms today, since it is illegal to discriminate in hiring because of the applicant's age.

Questions about the desired position, citizenship, company employment-related information, and so on, are all appropriate questions. It is doubtful, however, whether these should be positioned where they are on the form. The manager who is looking

Personal Data

Please Print In Ink

| Date |
| / / |

| Last Name | First Name or Initial | Middle Initial | Social Security Number |
| | | | — — |

| Street Address (Include City, State, and Zip Code) | Telephone No. (Inc. Area Code) |
| | ( ) |

If at present address for less than one year, list last previous address (include city, state, zip code)

Are you:
At least 18 years of age? ☐ Yes ☐ No
Under 70 years of age? ☐ Yes ☐ No

If under 18 years of age, applicant will be required to submit a work certificate if required by the state.

| If position requires use of car, do you have a valid driver's license ? ☐ Yes ☐ No | Position/general work area for which you are applying | Date you can start work / / |

Type of employment you are seeking
☐ Full Time ☐ Part Time ☐ Temporary

If part time or temporary, note days, hours, and length of time you desire employment

| Are you eligible to work in the United States ? ☐ Yes ☐ No | If you are not a citizen, list type of visa held | Document I.D. number |

| Have you previously applied for a position with us? ☐ Yes ☐ No | If "yes," note unit number and address | Date you applied for position / / |

| Have you ever been employed by us or any of our subsidiaries? ☐ Yes ☐ No | If "yes," note unit number and address | Termination date / / |

List relatives employed by us

Source of referral

☐ Advertisement ☐ Agency ☐ Personal ☐ Other (specify) _____

Indicate geographical area in which you would prefer to work

| First Choice | Second Choice |

Would you be willing to relocate wherever the company may assign you to work?

☐ Yes ☐ No

List any professional and business organizations to which you belong. You are not required to list any group or affiliation which may reveal your race, religion, sex or national origin.

Federal law and a majority of state laws prohibit discrimination in employment because of sex, race, color, religion, age, handicap, and national origin. The 1978 amendments to the Age Discrimination in Employment Act of 1967 prohibit discrimination on the basis of age with respect to individuals who are at least 40 but less than 70 years of age. Of course the company observes all valid state and local laws which have a higher age requirement.

FIGURE 7. A typical employment application form.

Education and Training

Circle Last Year Completed	Grade, Trade or High School												Technical - Business College					Graduate School			
	1	2	3	4	5	6	7	8	9	10	11	12	1	2	3	4	5	1	2	3	4

List Last High School and All Business, Trade Schools and Colleges Attended	Location (Include City and State)	Major	Minor	Degree Received	Cumulative Average (A, B, C, D)

Are you currently enrolled in evening, correspondence or other type of course study ?

☐ Yes ☐ No   If "yes," explain

Extracurricular activities (include offices held, scholarships, awards, honors, sports, hobbies, etc.)
You are not required to list any activities which may reveal your race, religion, sex, or national origin.

List any special skills and training

☐ Typing ☐ Steno ☐ Keypunch ☐ Business Machines ☐ Sales
☐ Other (Explain)

Do you have any physical or mental condition which may limit your ability to perform the job applied for or pose a potential risk to other employees ?

☐ Yes ☐ No   If "yes," explain

Have you been convicted of a felony involving dishonesty, breach of trust or one closely related to your future work here ?

☐ Yes ☐ No

I _____ acknowledge

(Print applicant's name and address)

that in connection with my application for employment, promotion or reassignment with this company, I have been advised in writing that an investigative consumer report may be made as to my character, general reputation, personal characteristics and mode of living. I authorize all persons, schools, companies, corporations and credit bureaus to supply information concerning my background.

I further acknowledge that I have been advised in writing by the company that upon written request within a reasonable time additional information as to the nature and scope of the report, if one is made, will be provided. This written request should be addressed to the personnel office where the application is filed.

I understand that if I am employed, any misrepresentation or omission of material facts on this application is sufficient cause for dismissal. My continued employment will depend upon the successful performance of work assigned to me and upon the further need of my continued employment by the company.

_____

(Signature of Applicant)

_____

(Date)

FIGURE 7 (*continued*)

Employment Experience - Include part time - cover the last five years, or previous three jobs. Start with present or most recent job.

Dates Employed	Company Name and Address	Positions Held	Salary	Reason for Leaving
From　／　／　To　／　／	Name Address Supervisor's Name	1 2 3	Initial $ Per Final $ Per	
From　／　／　To　／　／	Name Address Supervisor's Name	1 2 3	Initial $ Per Final $ Per	
From　／　／　To　／　／	Name Address Supervisor's Name	1 2 3	Initial $ Per Final $ Per	

Please use this space to elaborate on any background experience or other qualification which you believe should be considered in evaluating your qualifications for employment. Please indicate any aspects of prior military service which you would like considered in connection with your application for employment.

If currently employed, may we contact your employer for a reference at this time ?
☐ Yes　　☐ No

Is any additional information relative to change of name, use of assumed name or nickname necessary to enable a check on your work record?
☐ Yes　　☐ No

If "yes", explain

Name and address of person to contact in an emergency

FOR INTERNAL USE ONLY — DO NOT WRITE BELOW THIS LINE

TEST RESULTS

Clerical	Medical	Typing	Steno	Other

FIGURE 7 (*continued*)

for a competent worker is *most* interested in the applicant's work history, not in other information. Work history data, then, should come next on the form.

For the same reason, the manager will not want to see a list of the applicant's professional and business organization memberships *before* the work history has been provided. These less essential facts seem to have been located where they are on the employment application simply because whoever wrote the material decided that they should be included under the headings "Personal Data," "Education and Training," and "Employment Experience." Very little thought appears to have been given to what the manager making a final hiring decision will most need to see.

Next comes a section of questions about education and training. This section would be properly located if work experience questions preceded it. One heading, "Technical–Business College," is misleading, since it appears to exclude nonbusiness colleges and universities. Yet there is no other heading for this type of education.

Questions about possible criminal convictions seem out of place in an Education and Training section. Even more unusual is the fact that the firm asks the applicant to sign a statement guaranteeing the accuracy of information and acknowledging notification or investigation procedures *before* all employment history information has been completed. There is some question about whether the applicant could later claim that he or she believed that the accuracy guarantee applied *only* to information completed to that point.

The employment history information requested is adequate, although it might be more meaningful to leave the Reason for Leaving column blank for interviewer notes. As has already been mentioned, managers surveyed report that few people give their real reasons for leaving a job, and since their reasons are often subjective ones, the question may not be very helpful in finding competent workers.

"I use a Note column next to the employment history section," one manager reported. "Then I ask each applicant what his or her ex-supervisor is likely to say when I call to check on their references. Once that answer's given and noted, I ask why the applicant believes that's what the supervisor will say."

CHAPTER FOUR

Will you know a competent worker when you see one?

WILL YOU KNOW A COMPETENT WORKER WHEN YOU SEE ONE?

Competent workers exist, but to hire them you must recognize them when you see them. Unfortunately, no glowing sign saying "competent" lights up when you shake hands, and your task is left to your own ability to determine who is competent and who is not. Information from the top managers we interviewed and the traits identified in competent workers surveyed can provide some guidance.

"Look for professionalism, even if you're interviewing for a clerk-typist's position," one executive advises. She went on to say that the following are factors that she finds most often in competent workers:

A neatly and accurately prepared resume or work portfolio, even for a clerical job, and more advance portfolios for managerial applicants.

Neat appearance during the interview: a suit and tie for men, and neat business clothing for women (and an absence of excessive makeup and perfume).

An alert, interested, serious attitude. The applicant should ask intelligent questions about the work, as well as about hours, pay, and holidays.

A firm handshake—if any sort of aggressiveness is needed on the job.

Being on time, or early, for the interview.

Following up the interview with a letter, more work samples, or a telephone call expressing interest in the job and the company.

APPLICATIONS AS A GUIDE TO COMPETENCE

Through the use of the various parts of the employment application already discussed in Chapter 3, a complete application form has been put together that will provide additional guidelines to competence (see Figure 8).

In addition to knowing what information you want from this form, as explained in Chapter 3, managers surveyed suggested questions to ask as you go over the completed form with each applicant. We call this the Competence Questionnaire. Whether you use this questionnaire as a guide for your questions, or whether you write down the answers each applicant gives, make sure that you follow a standard routine in interviewing each applicant. This is required by law.

Begin with the section on personal information, making sure all information is complete. If it is not, ask why. "Some applicants who are still working will not record a work location or phone number for fear you'll call their boss," said one manager. "If they haven't given notice, that is a legitimate reason. But others won't record it because they don't want you to know they've been fired or asked to leave. You have to find out which it is."

The section on employment history is your key to identifying competent workers, according to the managers interviewed. If questions are not answered completely, ask for this information during the interview and record it. Next, ask the applicant what his or her most important skill has been on the current (or latest) job. Some managers interviewed recommend that the reply should match one of the skills you have listed in your job description for newspaper advertising (see Table 11, page 23).

Ask the applicant to outline the responsibilities he or she assumed (or carries out now), to determine whether he or she can handle responsibilities required for your vacant position. Assuming that survey results are an indication of a degree of compe-

APPLICATION FOR EMPLOYMENT

Name: _____

Home address (number, street, city, state): _____

_____

Home phone: _____

Work: Company name _____

　　　　Company address _____

Work phone: _____

May we contact you at work, if your application is discussed only with you?

_____ Yes _____ No

EMPLOYMENT HISTORY

Start with most recent job

Dates Began	Company name, address	Beginning salary	Immediate Supervisor	Summarize skills used, responsibilities
Left		Last salary	Company phone number	

Dates Began	Company name, address	Beginning salary	Immediate Supervisor	Summarize skills used, responsibilities
Left		Last salary	Company phone number	

Position wanted: _____

Describe the job skills, background, or training that might help you complete job tasks for the

position listed above. _____

_____

_____

Briefly state your job goals. _____

_____

_____

State highest level of education, last school attended, and grade point average. _____

_____

FIGURE 8. Suitable information to use on an application form.

tence, you may want to listen for words and phrases used by top-ranking survey respondents—words such as "accuracy," "completing needed work," "work speed," "dependability," and so on.

Even if you have read the applicant's information about skills and background, take a few minutes to ask in person for the same information. This will help you get to know the individual better.

Asking for this type of information can be difficult. Legally, the applicant is not required to tell you about his or her work attitudes, but must *volunteer* much of the information that will help you identify him or her as a competent worker. Perhaps the best approach is simply to ask the applicant to tell you about himself or herself and then listen carefully.

"If I hadn't asked that question in a recent interview, and then listened for 5 or 10 minutes instead of interupting with more questions, I'd never have known my applicant had been raised in a household containing three engineers," one manager said. "The fact that the applicant had no technical training or experience was hurting her chances for the job until that fact slipped into her conversation. I figured she'd been listening to engineering terms all of her life—at home. I was right, and she's working comfortably with technical data after only the briefest training."

Another manager, at the recommendation of a business associate, had interviewed an applicant who had no specific training for the opening. "The young man's degree wasn't related to the job at all," the manager said. "But he was so anxious to break into the industry. My associate told me the applicant's mother had worked in our industry for 18 years. I figured that he would at least have heard the terminology at home." (Ironically, the applicant started in the same kind of position his mother had held 18 years before.)

"His progress was very rapid," the manager reported, because he really understood the industry better than other young employees who *do* have job-related degrees."

During the interview, it is important to discuss the applicant's job goals. Managers interviewed confirmed survey results showing that the worker who puts pride in his or her work and who puts the enjoyment of work ahead of money is likely to be the more competent worker.

"That's not to say you can or should shortchange your workers with less-than-fair salaries," one manager said. "But their en-

---

COMPETENCE QUESTIONNAIRE

[Questionnaire to be used verbally in conjunction with the application form shown in Figure 8.]

1. Is all personal information completed? _____ Yes _____ No.

2. If not, why did applicant leave blanks?

3. Is work history information completed? _____ Yes _____ No.

4. What is your most important skill on your current (or latest) job?

5. Describe your responsibilities in your present (or latest) job.

6. Tell me about yourself.

7. Discuss the reasons you completed the job goals section as you did.

8. Tell me about your education.

FIGURE 9

joyment of their work should mean more to them than an extra $500 per year offered by a firm with a less interesting job."

"*Pride in work* and *importance of work* are phrases I listen for," an East Coast executive admitted. "In my experience, the use of those phrases almost always signals a competent employee."

More education does not necessarily mean more competence, survey results showed. Yet you should ask questions about educational information the applicant has provided. Again, let the applicant volunteer information if he or she will do so.

"You may find that the applicant went to a junior college instead of a top-ten school because she had to work her way through and could get a job locally," one manager told us. "Anyone who partially or totally works his way through school today will probably be a good worker in your operation, too."

TESTS HELP MEASURE COMPETENCE

Tests can help you pick out the most competent workers, but you must be sure those tests are legal before you use them. Many tests can be given by the hiring firm that cannot be legally used by employment agencies, simply because the government realizes that hiring companies are the only ones that know exactly what skills they need. Laws vary, however, and tests that are legal in one state may not be in another.

Federal law requires that all applicants be treated equally. This means that no matter what your state, you must test all applicants if you test any, and that the same test must be used for all. However, it is possible to give the test to all applicants who get as far as the second round of interviewing, which cuts down on the time spent in giving such tests.

Skills tests that are related to the skills needed for the job opening are legal even in the toughest states. Typists may be given typing and spelling tests, bookkeepers may be given math tests, and editors may be given editing tests, for example.

Aptitude tests are legal in many states, as a way to determine the applicant's abilities in selling, management, and so on.

Intelligence tests may be used in some states, provided a minimum IQ is set as a job requirement and provided all applicants are given the same test. A large Midwestern manufacturing company routinely gives all job applicants a Wonderlich test, for example. This requires only 12 minutes to complete.

"We don't use it for hiring criteria, but for job assignment criteria," the personnel manager said. "An applicant who scored 5 (50 is the top score possible) could never be given a job higher than that of sweeper, for instance."

An office manager, also in the Midwest, uses the same test. "I don't expect it to give perfect results," she said, "but a score of 20–30 means the applicant will do better—and be happier—in a more demanding job, such as executive secretary. With a lower score, the applicant might be better suited to less demanding work."

Personality tests are not used much today, although they are considered legal under some circumstances in some states. If the tests are used because the job criteria are that the employee have a stable personality, for example, the tests may be legal in some locations. "The trouble is that an intelligent person may know how to get around personality tests by giving you the answers you want to hear," one executive reminded us.

THE LAW: WHAT HAPPENS IF YOU BREAK IT?

"It may not be legal" is a phrase used by personnel people, by managers who interview, and sometimes by applicants who wanted a job that they didn't get.

If your operation is small, you may not be affected by some laws. Companies with fewer than five employees are subject to fewer regulations than are large firms.

Companies with no government contracts are subject to fewer regulations than those who hold such contracts. The regulations in question here are voluntary plans, as a rule.

If the Equal Employment Opportunities Commission approaches you, what happens will depend on what you did. If your violation was unintentional, a simple warning may be issued. If your firm has repeatedly violated the law, you may be taken to court.

Individuals may bring suits for discriminatory action, too. If they win, lost wages and damages may be awarded. But a suit can be won if you have honestly tried to treat applicants and employees equally and fairly, even if an individual applicant believes otherwise.

What about affirmative action programs? You may be asked to try to increase the percentage of minorities and women you hire. You may even find this helpful, since qualified women and minorities may work harder than other applicants to "prove" themselves. Particular pressure may be added to implement affirmative action programs if you have government contracts.

But at this writing, you cannot be *forced* to hire anyone. The EEOC may ask why various applicants were not hired. Be sure that you can show that all applicants were interviewed and tested in the same fashion. Ultimately, there should be no problem if you hire the most competent applicant available. It is still legal to hire the most competent applicant for your job.

CHAPTER FIVE

Search for applicants that are so good they'll replace you.

CHECKING ON COMPETENCE

Perhaps no area of hiring has come under greater fire than the checking of applicants' work references. Horror stories of lawsuits brought by ex-employees and a general unwillingness to say anything bad (outside the firm) about even the most incompetent worker have combined to make many reference checks worthless. Because of these factors many employers do not even attempt to make a reference check. Others make only a very superficial check, asking the personnel department to check the accuracy of employment dates.

The result of this unwillingness to check references is that more mediocre workers are hired than was true when references were thoroughly checked, according to managers interviewed.

Is reference checking legal? Of course it is. Attention should be given to this fact by the press to encourage ex-employers to speak up when they are called for a reference.

The phrasing of questions and answers is the key to legality. An ex-employer who deliberately and falsely maligns an ex-employee may be open to trouble, but the person who gives an honest evaluation of work performed and says it is his or her opinion, and not necessarily fact, violates no laws.

Can you, as a prospective employer, persuade the ex-employer that he or she should be open or honest with you about the applicant? This is where skill is required if you want an additional and very important guideline for checking the competence of someone you might hire.

SOME GUIDELINES FOR CHECKING COMPETENCE

One of the most important elements in checking references is to wait to make up your mind until *after* the phone calls, executives told us.

"Too often a manager only checks on one person—the one he's decided to hire," said one office supervisor. "Then he phrases the questions in such a positive way that the person called for the reference will usually just say, 'Sure, you're right. Mary was OK.' "

A better way, according to those interviewed, is to choose three "finalists." Draw up a list of pluses and minuses for each and add to those lists as you call for references. After completing all the calls for references, compare the three and make a final selection. "Put the ex-employer at ease by asking specific questions rather than vague ones," said another manager.

Some questions to ask when checking an applicant's references were the following:

How would you rate the applicant's work quality on a scale of 1–10, with 1 at the top?

What were the applicant's strongest work capabilities?

What were the applicant's weakest work performance traits?

Was the applicant absent or tardy more than once a month?

Why did the applicant leave the job previous to the last one?

If the applicant applied to you again, would you hire him or her?

What should the applicant have done to produce a better work record with the company?

Would you say the applicant's performance was better, the same, or not as good as other workers with the same responsibilities?

Other questions to ask should be related to specific work skills, such as how much experience the applicant has in operating a specific machine, how many pages of material he or she can type a day, and so on.

Some of the managers interviewed told us that they never call the reference listed on the application. If the applicant lists her immediate supervisor, they call the supervisor's boss. Or, alternatively, one company president suggested calling the people who worked for the applicant.

"You'll find out what sort of worker he or she is fast by doing that," he said.

"Applicants always put down a person who will give them a good reference," said another manager. "unless they've alienated absolutely everyone in the company."

It is important to check on entry-level applicants, too. If an applicant's record has holes that can't be checked, such as unexplained periods without a job or employers who are no longer in business, these may be warning signs.

Don't be afraid to spend money on a long-distance phone call if the applicant isn't local. For legal reasons, few ex-employers will reply to written requests for references, yet their opinions are vital in your search for the most competent worker.

TRIAL PERIODS AS A COMPETENCE CHECK

Most large companies have an informal three-month trial period to check competence. But if the employee is dismissed during this time, he or she may still be able to claim unemployment benefits against the company's account. A better method, where it can be used, is to give the applicants enough freelance or consulting work to be able to assess their competence.

At the entry level, college and university intern programs provide this kind of check. The individual works a specified number of hours or days for a semester or a school year. If he or she is very competent, the company will usually find a way to place him or her on the staff after the internship is completed.

Clerical help can be hired by using temporary clerical agency personnel until you find a competent worker who also wants a steady, full-time job. This will cost you a fee for the agency, but you'll know what type of worker you are hiring.

Managerial staff can often be hired only after successfully completing one or more consulting or freelance jobs with duties similar to those of the permanent position available.

GROUP HIRING AS A COMPETENCE CHECK

If the applicant will work for several individuals, or if the department requires more of a team than an individual effort, some managers will use group hiring as a competence check. "As many as four of us interview the three top applicants," one executive reported. "Then we discuss the advantages and drawbacks of each before a decision is made."

Group hiring doesn't always work, according to another manager. "We see the applicant and ask a few meaningless questions," she said, "but we can always tell who our boss wants, so naturally we vote for that applicant."

ADMIT YOUR MISTAKES

When you make a hiring mistake—and we all do—admit it and either retrain, move, or get rid of the incompetent worker. If it costs you unemployment money, it may be worth it.

"Our company is riddled with perfectly nice incompetent people no-one wanted to fire," said one supervisor. "Some have been doing mediocre jobs for 30 years, drawing ever-larger salaries for their 'long years of service' and pushing their work off onto others."

Mistakes can often be rectified by transferring an incompetent worker or by retraining him or her. "I hired a bright, fast typist to train for a junior management spot," said one executive. "She just couldn't retain what she was supposed to learn. Finally, I offered her a choice—dismissal or an executive secretary's spot with the chance to work her way up later when she'd proven herself. It was hard for her to take and hard for me to admit I'd made that error in judgement. We both learned a lesson."

Some workers might be competent in other jobs and will later be glad you fired them.

"We had a young writer who wanted to put together *New York Times* editorials," said one public relations agency manager. "But we write press releases about pumps here. This guy kept bringing environmental issues into play, and we finally let him go. I hope he makes it on a newspaper—that's where he belongs."

WEIGH COMPETENCE AND STABILITY

Put weight on the applicant's probable job stability as well as on his or her competence, said one manager interviewed. A bright, overqualified whiz may be able to do your job with one hand tied behind her back. But if there's nowhere to advance, she may be gone in a couple of months. This means you'll have to put out the time and money to find and train another new employee.

If the applicant *will* have room to advance, overqualification shouldn't be a problem. "I let the overqualified workers completely train the next person for that slot as a condition of advancement," reported one executive. "Lower-level employees see the chance for their own eventual advancement and work harder, too."

CHAPTER SIX

Good young workers are willing to "pay their dues" by taking low-level jobs as long as those jobs lead to something better.

WILL THE COMPETENT PERSON
ACCEPT YOUR JOB?

Finding competent workers is a difficult task, and once that's achieved you have an even greater challenge—making sure that he or she will accept the job you have to offer. Too many managers assume that because the applicant has agreed to an interview, he or she will take the job if it's offered. Not so. Actually, you must begin working at job acceptance *before* you begin interviewing applicants.

The first step is to take another look at what is most important to employees rated most competent in our survey. Family or love are the most important; the work itself ranks second. Money is least important, but this was so at least in part because the most competent workers also reported being paid at or above average rates. Thus, they assume payment will be good.

What can you do, then, to persuade competent workers to take your job? Since the employee's family or love life is (or should be) completely outside your realm, the most important thing you can do is to offer challenging work.

"I try to sell the job," says one office manager. "I need people who can solve work problems on their own without a lot of supervision. I make it clear that freedom to take on such work challenges and solve them is a big part of the job. The competent worker most often wants to stand on his or her own feet, and this approach is appealing."

CAREER ADVANCEMENT WINS "YES" ANSWERS

Competent workers usually are eager to advance their careers, and a good applicant is most likely to say yes to a job offer when career advancement possibilities are clear.

"Our department is supposed to have one secretary and one administrative assistant," reported a retailing chain manager. "Since I can't seem to find good secretaries for what our company is willing to pay, I've split the two jobs in half. I find competent new graduates willing to do clerical work half of the time so that they can learn business administration. At least once a year, one of these people can be promoted into a management trainee's spot, so they know ahead of time that the clerical work won't last forever if they can prove their worth."

"It's called 'paying your dues,' " quipped the managing editor of an international magazine. "I started out at the bottom and took the jobs that would let me grow. The most competent kids today will do the same thing. Be wary of the young grad who's 'above' writing beginning assignments and wants to start in on editorials the first week."

"It's important to back up your career advancement plans with concrete work 'plums,' " executives interviewed said.

"I make it clear that once the secretarial load is finished for the day, the employee can work on press release writing," said one public relations account executive. "That usually means that the competent worker will finish the dull clerical work rapidly, in order to spend more time on the writing he or she really wants to do."

"Be sure that time really exists for the interesting part of the job," cautioned another manager.

Career growth is perhaps even more important to the middle-management workers being hired. "I tell competent applicants that I want them to be so good that they'll replace me—and I mean it," reported a retail chain executive. "I don't want to stay in my job forever, and I can't climb if there isn't someone here to fill my shoes."

"The best prospective employees have to be able to see at least one future move up the career ladder, or they'll take a different job—even if it means a lower salary," reported an office manager.

CO-WORKERS: ANOTHER WAY TO SELL THE JOB

Although not ranked first or second co-workers are an important element in selling a job. Many of us make friends at work, and even find mates there. This is hardly surprising since we spend a good percentage of our waking hours at work. You can test this theory for yourself by making a list of the ten friends you currently see most often and noting where you met them.

"I'm from the Midwest," said one East Coast manager. "That means that almost all of my friends—and my wife—were originally work contacts. I remember this fact when I'm hiring. The people should be able to get along well together."

"It raises the chances of getting a 'yes' to a job offer if the applicant meets his or her prospective co-workers and likes them," reported another executive.

Such meetings can be totally informal or over lunch. One publisher asks the prospective employee to sit in on the weekly editorial meeting where personalities, the way work problems are handled, compliments, and criticisms all come out in the open.

"Likes attract," reported an office manager. "If a competent worker sees other bright, hard-working people in the office, the answer is more likely to be 'yes.'"

A plethora of incompetent workers may prevent your hiring new, good workers, too. "The good applicants take one look at the take-your-time attitude of my assembly-line workers, and don't take the job," reported a frustrated factory foreman. "If by chance they do take the job, they don't last long. The pace is too boring."

MONEY: IT MATTERS

Money matters in getting a "yes" from the job applicant you want to hire. Even though it is not an important element when it is adequate, according to survey results, it quickly becomes vital when it is not sufficient.

"Good workers generally assume they will be paid fairly," reported one manager, "and they leave if they're not."

Some rules were outlined by managers responding to our survey, to provide a guide to money's role in hiring competent workers:

Never ask a prospective employee to take a cut in pay. Even if the work is more interesting and will eventually lead to a better, higher-paying job, a cut in pay almost always leads to worker dissatisfaction and resentment.

If possible, offer the prospective employee a little more money than requested. This shows good faith in the individual's ability.

Hire competent workers in lower-salary range groups to meet your budget. If your salary range is $12,500–$14,000, don't interview people who want more. It is legal to use this approach, as long as you pay the same salary for the same work to everyone you hire.

Inform the prospective worker of benefits and their annual value, but don't depend on benefits to obtain your "yes." Good workers expect adequate health insurance and retirement plans. Although they might be dissuaded from a job without benefits, benefits in themselves are not likely to encourage them to take a specific job.

When pay controls are in effect or are likely, whether voluntary or mandatory, start the worker at the highest salary possible. It may be easier than fighting for the big raise—vastly exceeding guidelines—that you will need to keep the competition from hiring your best people.

PHYSICAL SURROUNDINGS MAKE A DIFFERENCE

Pleasant surroundings can encourage a good worker to take your job offer. Be sure to show the applicant where he or she will work.

"I learned that lesson through one of my own interviews," said one retail manager. "I received a great offer moneywise, but I was hesitating because I liked the job I had. Then, I saw my proposed workplace—a bullpen-type arrangement with three other managers, and the offices weren't very nice overall. I thought about my own pleasant office with its window and good location, and I turned down a $5,000 increase."

Even if you can't offer the most posh surroundings to workers, do consider the best physical arrangement. "My salespeople have to share offices because we're out of space," said a West Coast sales manager. "But I try to match personalities so that the two in an office get along with each other."

SHOW A PERSONAL INTEREST

A prospective employee will be more likely to take your job offer if he or she can tell that you care about your workers and their success. You can't fake this and expect it to work; you must genuinely care about them as individuals and as workers. If you don't, perhaps you shouldn't be in management.

If you do have the advantage of being a caring boss, don't be afraid to show it.

CHAPTER SEVEN

Fight corporate policy when it's keeping you from finding or using a good worker.

THE EFFECTS OF COMPANY SIZE

Whether you are a manager in a small company or an executive in a large corporation, the size of your firm affects the type of worker who will most happily work for you, what you can do with that worker, and many other elements of your operation.

In our survey and interviews, we included a good cross section of company sizes, from mom-and-pop operations to firms ranking in the top three in their industry. Replies of managers interviewed show that a competent worker in a small firm may not perform well on the corporate scene; and the reverse is true, too. It's a matter of personalities and inclinations, methods of work, patience, and other factors.

SMALL FIRMS' ADVANTAGES AND COMPETENCE

The small company has many advantages when it comes to hiring competent employees. If it is small enough, it may be free from many government pressures that affect large corporations, including the requirements for obtaining government contracts, such as affirmative action programs, the need to follow voluntary government wage guidelines to hold onto government contracts, and so on.

In a smaller company, managers reported that they are relatively free of restrictions set by lawyers working for the company and other hierarchical restrictions that gradually accumulate in the makeup of a large corporation.

"Albert Ellis says we 'must' ourselves beyond the limits of rationality," quipped one computer company manager. "That's why I got out of the big corporation and into a small company. I was tired of trying to meet a list of 427 things I *must* or *must not* do each day."

When hiring—or using—good workers, the small company can offer them more flexibility, more money (if profits will support this), and usually a more comradely, closely-knit work atmosphere.

"I would never work for a large company again," reports the field manager of a small construction firm. "I tried that. I got paid the same as all of the other supervisors even though I did twice the work. Here, we use subcontractors and I am the supervisor. If I work like hell, and our profits double, the owner gives me a big chunk. I don't have to ask, and the government can't tell him to limit it to 8.5% because we have no government contracts."

Some small companies purposely give each employee a different job title—not difficult with only a limited number of workers and managers.

"It helps us stay out of the box of 'same salaries,' " admitted one small business owner. "An employee can't sue for wage discrimination on any basis if he or she is the only employee at that level. It then becomes a simple matter of their leaving if they don't like what they're paid."

"Many good workers like the idea of being part of a small, growing company," one manufacturer reported. "They can see tangible results of their work quickly, and it is reflected in our growth. That's a strong point to make when you're looking for competent workers."

Flexibility of hours and duties are apt to attract some competent workers to a small firm, too. "My keypunch operator was turned down by a large firm," chuckled a small firm's manager. "She wanted to work only six hours a day, and they have a corporate policy against permanent part-timers. She does more than a full day's work in those six hours, so their rules are great for me."

"My secretary's top-notch," reported the owner of a small factory. "She left a large company because she had to keep the time sheet and she said it made her feel like the office snitch. Originally, that was part of her job here, too. But we all sign ourselves in and out now."

Some competent workers prefer small companies for all sorts of reasons. In addition to those already mentioned, the absence of a formal dress code was one that workers indicated.

"I have a great bookkeeper who comes to work in jeans, which he couldn't do in his previous job with a large company," said one manager. "There's no good reason he should have to wear a suit: The customers don't see him, so why should I care."

"I think people work harder in a small company," reported one business owner. "It's very obvious what everyone is or isn't doing in a small company. The work becomes a matter of pulling together as a team if the company is to grow. In a big firm or in government, it's easier to get lost in the shuffle."

LARGE FIRMS' ADVANTAGES AND COMPETENCE

Large companies have advantages to offer competent workers, too, and the most obvious is stability. Competent workers, like any employees, prefer not to have to worry about whether the company will fold, leaving them jobless. Large corporations can often afford to pay top salaries and offer the best benefits, which can attract competent employees. The catch is that top starting salaries and stability will attract all sorts of applicants, and individual managers must then work at finding the most able workers.

One decided advantage that large corporations have in attracting good employees is that there should almost always be room for workers to move up the career ladder. Such upward movement may be stopped by departmental structure or office politics, however.

Some large corporations offer good mobility from department to department by means of job-posting techniques.

"We get a crack at any job for which we're qualified," reports one middle-management employee in a large insurance company. "All jobs are posted by title, grade, and salary *before* they're advertised on the outside."

This kind of mobility, plus the assurance of equal pay for equal work, is a strong selling point when offering a job to a competent worker who might be paid less in a small company without job grade and salary protection.

"I like to hire good workers when they're ready to settle into a career spot," said one executive of a large firm. "Usually, they've moved a few times for growth or more money, but are starting to think about putting in at least their last 20 years in one spot to have good retirement benefits. You have to be sure they also want to continue to advance, and aren't just looking for a comfortable niche, though."

THE BEST OF LARGE AND SMALL COMPANIES

Perhaps the manager who can most easily hire competent employees is the one who has created the best of both worlds—a small, fairly autonomous department within the secure structure of a large corporation. If this is your goal, you must realize that you don't create such a department by accident.

"You start by being willing to fight corporate policy when it's keeping you from finding or using good workers, or when it's keeping you from getting your job done," one exporting firm executive said. "This means that you must have the corporate political connections necessary to break corporate policy, and that those lateral to you in other departments that affect you *know* you can do what you want even if you have to get permission from your superior. Once they know you *can* get such permission, they'll usually let you do what you want without it."

Managers who have established small-business-type departments within large companies usually let the departments run internally as if they were independent operations.

"My department heads make their decisions and tell me why," said one divisional manager. "If the reasons are right, I say 'yes' immediately and then they go ahead. I do the fighting with top management and get the okay three months later. If we had to wait for three months, all of the enthusiasm would be gone—and so would my best department heads."

Getting around corporate pay policies is essential for the department-in-a-corporation operation. "You've got to be willing to pay a good worker as much as or more than can be had elsewhere. Change the title and job duties if you want someone the corporation says you can't afford," one executive recommended. "Make the job a grade 17 by adding some new duties, rather than sticking to the grade 15 that was authorized—and then be prepared to tell top management why your department *needs* the revised job in order to operate profitably."

If you want to hire all top people and pay them more, how can you meet corporate budgets? "Either expand operations or reduce the total number of people," one manager replied. "I'd rather have six good people than ten mediocre ones—and work gets done faster that way, too. But you can open new units or start spin-offs of your operation, and the new profits will justify the better people and salaries you want."

"Competent workers are attracted to a growing, dynamic department or division within a large corporation," said a West Coast wholesaler. "If you can show this kind of operation to a good job applicant, the answer to the job offer is likely to be 'yes.' "

CHAPTER EIGHT

PROFITING FROM COMPETENT
PEOPLE IN SALES

No area of business shows an employee's competence or incompetence more quickly than sales. A salesperson's performance can be easily measured in dollars and compared with the performance of other salespeople who have similar territories or with the performance of the previous salesperson in the same territory.

Until recent years, many salespeople worked on straight commission—that is, they were paid only when they made sales. Very few salespeople are paid on this basis today, and even top sales managers seem to accept that a salary-plus-commission plan is here to stay. Is this necessarily so?

"No-one will work on a straight commission basis," one East Coast sales manager said.

"Not so," replied a Midwestern retailer. "If you provide a commission that will allow a higher income once sales pass a certain level, the good salesperson will prefer straight commissions."

Firing salespeople for inadequate performance has gone out of style as a method of motivation, too. Only a few years ago, a large food and housewares chain that sold door-to-door organized its salespeople into ten-person districts. At the end of the year, the three lowest producers were dismissed from each team—no matter what their sales and no matter how long they had been with the company.

Such tactics may still be used by small firms to keep salespeople producing, but larger companies have adopted other methods of motivation.

MOTIVATING THE INSIDE SALESPERSON

Inside selling, or clerking in a store, is quite different from outside selling, or calling on customers in their homes or offices. Different types of workers are competent at these different kinds of sales, and different types of motivation are needed, according to managers interviewed.

"Inside selling is easier," one West Coast retailer explained. "This is so because the customer comes to you. This means that he or she wants something similar to the products you stock, while the outside salesperson may be trying to move merchandise to some one who neither wants nor needs it."

This means that you can hire a friendly, helpful person for an inside sales job, while someone with a more aggressive personality may be needed for outside selling.

Hiring should be completed as for any other job, after checking applicant training, experience, and professionalism. If anything, hiring a competent salesperson should be easier than hiring for positions where past performance is harder to measure.

Motivating the inside salesperson, once he or she is on the job, involves several elements, according to the managers we interviewed.

"Money incentives have the strongest motivating power, since salespeople expect to receive incentive payments," according to an executive with one of the top three U. S. retail chains. A variety of incentive elements should be combined for the best overall plan, and here is what this executive recommends:

Pay a base salary that is about two-thirds of what the average inside salesperson expects to earn.

Set a quota that equals about 20 times the base salary. Thus, if the salesperson has a base salary of $150 per week, his or her quota might be $3,000 worth of sales per week. Price differences in merchandise will be taken care of largely by volume of sales, since large-ticket items are not frequently purchased, but adjustments can be made for this factor if necessary.

Use a sliding commission that *increases* as sales volume goes up. Using the 5% above as a base, salespeople might be paid 5.5% on the first $500 of sales over their quota; 6% on the next $500 of sales over quota; and so on. Following this pattern, the earnings of a salesperson with weekly sales of $4,500 would be as shown in the following table:

Base salary (sales to $3,000)	$150.00
Commissions at 5.5% on sales from $3,000 to $3,500	27.50
Commissions at 6% on sales from $3,500 to $4,000	30.00
Commissions at 6.5% on sales from $4,000 to $4,500	32.50
Total wages and commissions	$240.00

Occasionally put special incentives on hard-to-move merchandise. You can use either a flat bonus per item sold or a small additional commission. One store paid $0.50 extra per unit on designer jeans, for example, when the manager found the store was heavily overstocked with the merchandise.

Arrange for incentives to be paid as *frequently* as possible—the motivation is stronger if payment will be soon.

Training is also essential to motivating inside salespeople. The salesperson should learn both new selling techniques and facts about the merchandise to be sold.

"Just as an author should write about what he or she knows, a salesperson should only sell products that he or she understands," advises a Midwestern ladies-wear retailer. "If my clerks don't understand what styles and colors look best on specific types of figures, I teach them. I teach them to guide women to the garments that will make them look best, to use compliments *only* when the customer tries on a dress or suit that really does make her look better. We have weekly sessions to look at new merchandise and to discuss which accessories will go well with it. You'd be surprised how much sales go up when each dress or suit purchase is accompanied by an accessory purchase."

"Employees must be trained to look at our display windows

and then be sure they're familiar with the merchandise in them," a hardware dealer told us. "A housewife may be intrigued by an electric wok in the window, but it's up to the salesperson to make the sale by explaining the advantages of the appliance."

"An employee who waits for the customer to find merchandise and hand it over is a cashier, not a salesperson," said one retail store manager. "This principle works in self-service stores where customers may make buying mistakes to get a lower price. Actually, a knowledgeable salesperson who can provide information and advice about products can save the customer money even at a higher merchandise price."

If you doubt that this is true, think about your own closet, kitchen cabinet, or garage. How many shirts or pairs of shoes that don't really fit, dishes that have no use, or useless do-it-yourself gadgets have you bought in a self-service store because the price was low?

"There's nothing wrong with teaching inside salespeople some basic selling techniques," quipped one department manager. "It makes them realize they're supposed to be selling rather than just collecting money."

Basic selling steps that can be taught include:

facts about the merchandise,

advantages of the merchandise,

ways to present the merchandise to the customer in a positive way,

the importance of being friendly and helpful to all customers (the customer is *still* always right in good selling), and

the need to ask for the business.

This last step is essential for both inside and outside salespeople. No matter how thoroughly the salesperson discusses a product, until he or she says, "Is that the model you'd like?" or "Which of the two machines do you want?" or "If you'd like both suits, I can give you 10% off on the second one," no sale will be made.

"*Competition* among salespeople can also serve as a good motivator," said a Los Angeles retailer. "This is true for inside and outside selling."

Competition, according to this executive, should be set up within each department so that salespeople are selling against those selling same-price-ticket merchandise. Sales results of the top performers, if not the results of each salesperson, should be listed where co-workers will see them, perhaps in the company cafeteria. Some stores even send sales results to salespeople at home, to get their families involved in the competition.

Prizes are necessary if there is to be serious competition among salespeople. These prizes can consist of cash, merchandise or (over an extended period of selling) trips. It may be necessary to experiment to determine whether small, frequent competitions work best in a specific store, or whether longer, large-prize competitions are the most effective motivators.

"Management acknowledgment is the forgotten incentive," reported a small Midwestern shopowner. "But I'm reminded when I tell a salesperson that he or she is doing a great job and get a smile—and even better work—in return."

Praise costs nothing except a few minutes of the manager's time, and should be handed out in liberal doses whenever it is deserved—in outside or inside selling.

MOTIVATING THE OUTSIDE SALESPERSON

Commissions are the most commonly used method of motivating outside salespeople—those that sell directly to the buyer in his or her home or office. This kind of selling is more difficult than selling in a store, because the salesperson often cannot be sure that the prospect wants to buy anything. Thus, outside selling is generally rewarded with higher commissions or some other payment.

The difficulty of outside sales also depends on the product. Intangible products, such as life insurance, are usually considered the most difficult and usually carry the highest commission rates for selling.

"Money should be the best motivator," said one sales manager interviewed. "If I had my way, I'd pay no base salary and use only good commissions."

Setting Up a Commission Plan. A commission-only payment plan is generally not used today, except when employing outside representatives. Since this is so, how can you establish a commission system that will motivate? The following guidelines were established by an international sales manager interviewed after initial survey results were completed.

Begin by deciding what total sales costs should be. In our case, we pay sales reps 20%, so we try to keep total sales costs of company salespeople to about the same amount.

I set up our program by looking at past sales of our sales staff. Average sales per person were $300,000. This meant that total cost per salesperson—base salary, expense accounts, benefits (including a company car), office space, and commissions for his account of sales—should not exceed $60,000.

Office space per salesperson costs about $3,000 in our location. Benefits, including a company car, cost about $5,500 per year. Expense accounts average $30,000 per salesperson. This gave me a base cost of about $38,500 per salesperson. To that, I added a base salary of $18,000, which is the minimum these days—even for a young salesperson. This brought me to a total of $56,500 per salesperson.

With this figure, the salesperson must sell $272,500 before his or her "cost" is 20%. If I hire a more experienced salesperson and pay a larger base, the breakeven point must be adjusted, of course. For example, if I gave a $30,000 base, the total cost for that person would rise to $68,500, and sales needed to break even with sales costs at 20% would be $342,000 per year.

But the real goal is to reduce sales costs *below* 20%, while *increasing* sales.

Once I've calculated the breakeven figure as explained above, I add 10% to cover salespeople who do not reach their goals, and set the figure as the salesperson's quota. In the first example, the annual sales quota would be $300,000 (rounded off), and in the second example, the quota would be $400,000.

Because motivational returns should be given as quickly as possible, I split these quotas into quarterly figures. This means that the first salesperson's sales quota is $75,000 per quarter, while the second person's quota is $100,000 per quarter.

Next, salespeople earn additional commissions on sales made *over* their quotas. It is absolutely essential that these commissions increase as sales volume goes up. Companies that pay a stationary or a decreasing percentage will never be able to hire or keep the best salespeople.

I begin by paying an additional 6% on the first $25,000 above each quarter's quota or each $100,000 annually. Remember that expenses such as car mileage and expense account spending will go up, too, as the aggressive salesperson makes more calls.

If the salesperson passes $50,000 in excess of the quarterly quota, *all* commissions over the quota are set at 8%.

If the salesperson sells $75,000 more than the quarterly quota, *all* commissions for the quarter are paid at 10%.

Percentages and volumes will vary tremendously from industry to industry, but this basic plan can be adapted to your operation if you estimate average cost of selling as a percentage of sales and alter the plan to this percentage.

Contests Can Motivate. Sales contests are probably the second most common sales motivator. If you use them, be sure to figure their costs into the total cost of selling, and adjust base salaries and commissions accordingly.

Managers interviewed reported that sales contests are most successful when these steps are taken:

The prize is really large enough to be attractive.

The prize also appeals to the salesperson's spouse or family.

Top management makes it clear that results will affect the salesperson's record or future with the company.

Contest rules are established that truly give each salesperson—not just the person in the best territory—a chance to win.

Interim results are provided frequently, including sending these to the salesperson's spouse, secretary, assistant, and so on.

If several prizes are given, motivation will increase.

Interim prizes (weekly) may be given, with the final prize awarded at the end of a month-long contest, for example.

A promotional campaign to encourage the salesperson to work at the contest can help results. Such a campaign is conducted much as a direct-mail campaign is used with buying prospects. In effect, you're selling your salespeople on the idea of selling for you.

Training is an Often-Forgotten Motivational Key. If you're working with experienced salespeople, you'd better find another name for what must be done. Call it sales meetings, sales brainstorming, or anything else you like. But don't lose sight in your own mind of the fact that even the most experienced salespeople must be trained and retrained. So say the sales managers interviewed. Why is this necessary? Except for a few very self-motivated individuals who are always developing new selling techniques, most salespeople get stale and depend on comfortable selling relationships for the bulk of their business.

"The most important part of training salespeople is making sure they know the advantages of their product," said one sales manager. "I make periodic calls with each individual and give the sales pitch, to refresh the salesperson's memory as to product advantages."

"It's important that the salesperson feel free to ask for help," reported another executive. "I've taught my sales staff to call me or my assistant and say, 'I need help! I didn't know how to answer a prospect's objections to my products. What could I have said?' We discuss the whole conversation, and the salesperson immediately makes another call, or at least writes a letter, answering the objections."

An important part of training is making sure that all salespeople have the available sales tools and know how to use them. In one company, supplies of sales tools (catalogs, data sheets, and so on) were sent to salespeople as soon as printed. A new salesman joined the staff, taking over for a retiring salesman in the Denver territory. After six months, he mentioned rather wistfully that a catalog would be better than the three-year-old product sheet he was using.

"What?" the sales manager exploded over the phone. "We sent a supply of new catalogs to Denver eight months ago!"

Perhaps the retiring salesman used all of the catalogs; perhaps he pitched them in the wastepaper basket as he cleaned out his desk. The point is that each new salesperson should be trained as if he or she had no sales tools and knew nothing about the product. (The sales manager of this company told us that he now makes training calls with each new salesperson and hand-delivers that person's supply of each sales aid. Reorders of the selling tools are left to the salesperson.)

Role playing can be an effective sales training tool, said a number of the sales managers interviewed. Ask the salesperson to play the part of his or her toughest customer, while you play the role of the salesperson. Lessons in why prospects object to buying are bound to be learned.

Prospecting training is an important area, too. "My salespeople made plenty of calls, but didn't sell much," one sales manager complained. "Then we started training the sales staff how to pinpoint companies with a real need for our products—and how to find the one individual who can say 'yes' inside those firms. Without qualifying prospects in that way, too much time is wasted."

"Some prospecting tricks are so easy to teach salespeople," said a West Coast executive "For example, he or she can easily ask a customer which firms are considered their main competition. The customer will construe the question as an interest in the business, but the reply provides the salesperson with some top-quality prospects."

"You can do the same thing with the Yellow Pages," added this executive's assistant. "Have the salesperson look up the customer's product category. Generally, firms with display ads for that product are the best prospects."

"Or, salespeople can read their customer's trade magazines," the executive countered. "They'll see all sorts of new project announcements, keep up with promotions of buying-level executives, and so on."

By far the most important training for salespeople is in how to close a sale, according to sales managers interviewed. This seems an elementary fact, yet many experienced salespeople do not really know how to close.

"Absolutely nothing happens until you ask for the order," says one executive. "You can teach your staff a hundred closing lines, but make *sure* they know at least a few."

Salespeople should use a positive approach in asking for business, managers interviewed agreed. "I really didn't think about the importance of closings until I actually heard a salesman say on the phone, 'You wouldn't like to buy another case of the Sauterne you enjoyed before, would you?' I hit the roof! He could have said, 'Would you like to take advantage of our special price on a case of the Sauterne that you enjoyed before?' or 'The Sauterne's in at a good price. Should I put you down for a case?' He didn't, and I guess it was my fault for not teaching him the right way to close."

"Teaching salespeople to close is tricky," reported another executive. "They can't be too flip or high pressure. A little humility can help in closing."

This manager went on to describe two advertising space salesmen who call on him. "One breezed in with 'and how much are you upping your ad budget for us this year?' In fact, I *was* increasing the total advertising budget, but I didn't like his attitude and I cut what I spent with him in half—all in the space of 30 seconds.

"The second salesman explained his magazine and why he thought it would help us achieve our goals and then asked, 'Will you give us a chance to prove that we can do the job for you?' Needless to say, that fellow got most of my budget."

Appreciation Is a Good Motivator. By nature, the sales personality is an outgoing one. "If you can make a salesperson feel very important and very appreciated when he or she succeeds, you'll find a lot more sales effort exerted," reported a Midwestern sales manager.

"We have company awards and plaques to help boost the sales ego," responded one executive, "but nothing is more effective than the manager's being sure to hand out deserved praise."

"Praise and reassurance are needed, even when the salesperson isn't doing well," said another manager. "If you say, 'you can do it, just keep trying'—and keep repeating that message—it can make all the difference in the world to a salesperson who's temporarily in the doldrums."

"Praise doesn't cost a cent," said another manager. "Yet it can get better results than extra money where salespeople are involved. Few salespeople hear praise from their customers, so it's doubly important to hear it from their boss."

Punishments as Motivators. Some managers use the stick end of the carrot-and-stick motivation technique, but few felt that this was very effective. "If you've really tried to train, inspire, and motivate a salesperson who flops, the only real answer is to fire him or her and try again," said one sales manager.

The only place for punishments as motivators may be when dismissal is not possible. "After a salesperson's been on the staff for five years, it's almost impossible to fire him or her," reported an executive in a large corporation. "The company disapproves. This means that requiring detailed sales reports, questioning expense accounts, and other 'punishments' are the only ways to deal with the problem of a nonproductive salesperson."

"I sell my nonproductive salespeople," chuckled a manager in a large corporation that also frowns on firing long-timers. "I persuade other managers in the company—or outside it—to look at the advantages the person has. I don't mention the problems. Usually, someone will hire them away from me. Now, that's selling!"

A MOTIVATIONAL CHECKLIST

The tactics we have discussed to motivate salespeople are brought together in the following checklist.

Pay as much of the total wage as possible in the form of commissions.

Hold competitions.

Train salespeople as to product or service advantages.

Provide adequate sales aids, advertising, and backup services.

Provide a good-quality product or service so that the salesperson can count on multiple sales.

Praise the salesperson when praise is deserved.

Train even experienced salespeople in basic prospecting, presentation, and closing techniques to keep them on their toes.

Fire salespeople who can't meet quotas after a fair trial period.

CHAPTER NINE

PROFITING FROM COMPETENT OFFICE WORKERS

It may be harder to find competent office workers than any other type of employee, according to the interviews conducted with managers nationwide. There are many reasons. Good workers often prefer challenging, interesting work, which office work may not be. The status that accompanies office work also leaves something to be desired.

Whatever the problems of finding competent office workers, managers agree: "Once you've found a good office worker, work hard to keep him or her happy."

That comment carries one clue to successful hiring—look at male clerical workers, as required by law. While women workers are eager for jobs that carry more status, growing numbers of men look at office work as a relatively pressure-free environment and a way to make a fair living. The use of male typists and stenographers is more widespread on the East and West Coasts, but is spreading across the country.

"One interesting factor is that young men are taking office jobs to get a foot in the door and work their way up," said one office manager. "These fellows who apply have superior skills most of the time—they can type 70 or 80 words per minute—but this is not always the case. Last week, I couldn't hire a really bright guy—his typing was just too slow."

MONEY: ONLY ONE FACTOR

Top dollars may help you hire a competent office worker, and you probably will not be able to hire the person you need without an average or better salary to offer. But you should always realize that the money is *expected*, and other factors will be largely responsible for motivating and keeping the best office worker. This is not to understate the value of an adequate wage. And we repeat—without this, you will probably not be able to hire a competent office worker.

What is an adequate wage? Interviews across the country revealed office salaries to be more uniform than in any other job area. In contrast, college graduates with journalism degrees were offered less than the average starting salary for typists by New York City newspapers. We were told that these applicants not only accept these low salaries, but feel lucky to have any job at all in their chosen field.

A more skilled and experienced office worker can earn as much as a management trainee with a college degree in large cities, especially in the East. Executive secretaries and administrative assistants may earn much more.

All of this means that, unless you own and operate your own business, you probably cannot offer enough additional money to office workers to make money a factor in whether they stay on the job or go elsewhere. Only if the expected money is *not* available will money become a factor.

The shortage of office workers, by the way, may not be a problem that lasts indefinitely. As computerized word processing equipment is developed and becomes more sophisticated, and as office work becomes more automated, the market for office workers may change.

WORK AND RESPONSIBILITY BALANCING

Assuming that your company will not let you pay a middle-management level salary for an office employee, work and responsibility balancing may be the best method to motivate and retain competent office workers. Work and responsibility balancing means that you take a dull, routine job and a more interesting job and split the work in half so that each of two workers has enough challenging work to ease the malaise that a good worker feels when having to do very routine, dull work.

"I tried hiring a clerk-typist to do our basic routine office work," one manager told us. "It was not possible to find a good worker for the salary my company allows us to pay clerk-typists. I took an administrative assistant's job, and split the duties 50–50 for both positions. Each of the two workers now gets 50% routine work, 50% challenging work, as well as a chance to move up the career ladder."

Fields that can most successfully use the work- and responsibility-balancing technique are those that are most overcrowded, and which have large numbers of entry-level applicants who are unable to find jobs within the industry. These individuals may then be willing to take the office-type position in the hope of being promoted to a more professional position later. Currently, these overcrowded fields include psychology, television, journalism, and so on.

"Entry-level research jobs in psychology are almost impossible to find," said the head of one university psychology department. "At the same time, I find it impossible to hire a good clerk-typist for $175 per week, as allowed. I combine the two jobs, giving each person half office-work duties and half research duties, paying $160 per week. And I am absolutely inundated with applicants each time I advertise—some with PhDs."

Is it possible to keep these highly educated individuals in a job if they are hired under work- and responsibility-balancing conditions? "On the average, I keep such employees at least two years—and longer if I'm able to promote them," said one manager. "But even if the average were only six months, I'd rather have competent workers for a short time than hire poor workers who stayed forever."

Will workers devote as much energy to the office-work half of their jobs as to their more interesting duties, under a work- and responsibility-balancing plan?

"Absolutely!" replied a newspaper editor. "I make it clear that once the clerical work is completed, the remaining time can be spent on writing. Usually, they work very hard to complete the office work in *less* than 50% of the work day."

WORK REORGANIZATION IS A KEY TO PRODUCTIVITY

Another key to office work productivity and stability is reorganization of duties to fit individual skills. "I had a fairly good typist who was really sharp with figures," said one manager. "When my contract control recordkeeper left, I gave the figure work to my typist and hired a new person with typing skills for some of her old duties. The new employee had enough math ability to serve as a backup."

"I hired an administrative assistant who is an excellent photographer," said another office manager. "She's doing all of the photos for our promotional materials—this helps keep her happy and provides us with better photographs than our promotion department ever took."

Even within a job, where no work division is possible, productivity can be increased by varying the duties. "Instead of dictating for hours, I let my secretary work at other tasks periodically to break the monotony," one executive reported. "If I give her my dictation tape each day, she can usually finish that element of her work in an hour or so—much better than if she has to type letters all day because I let the dictation pile up."

"Phone answering is of key importance in our office," said a West Coast executive. "So I assign the work to someone with the ability to handle our small interoffice board *and* with an outgoing personality. Getting the job done right is more important than whose job it is *supposed* to be."

INTEROFFICE RELATIONSHIPS

Interoffice relationships can help competent workers get more accomplished, or they can stand in the way of accomplishment. Which direction relationships take often is the result of managerial policies and personalities, according to executives interviewed. The direction can almost always be affected by management.

How can you, as a manager, create an office atmosphere that will help competent workers do more and better work? Recommended one office manager in a small Midwestern manufacturing plant,

Begin by honestly assessing your staff. There will always be one or two less competent people or people with disruptive personalities that you had to hire—either for company political reasons or for lack of more suitable applicants at the time. Or, maybe you're new and you inherited some employees you wouldn't have hired had the decision been yours.

Once you've made an evaluation—on paper, if necessary—do a quick office layout and see where these disruptive personalities are located. For example, if you have an office gossip, or an individual who makes a lot of personal phone calls, he or she should be put in as isolated a location as possible to keep him or her from wasting the time of your good workers.

I inherited a situation of this type and quickly noticed that good workers were being prevented from working by an individual. Most of them were also resentful that the disruptive person got

FIGURE 10. Dotted line shows location of 5-foot-high dividers that were used to give "privacy" to an administrative assistant with a disruptive personality and to keep him from wasting the time of co-workers.

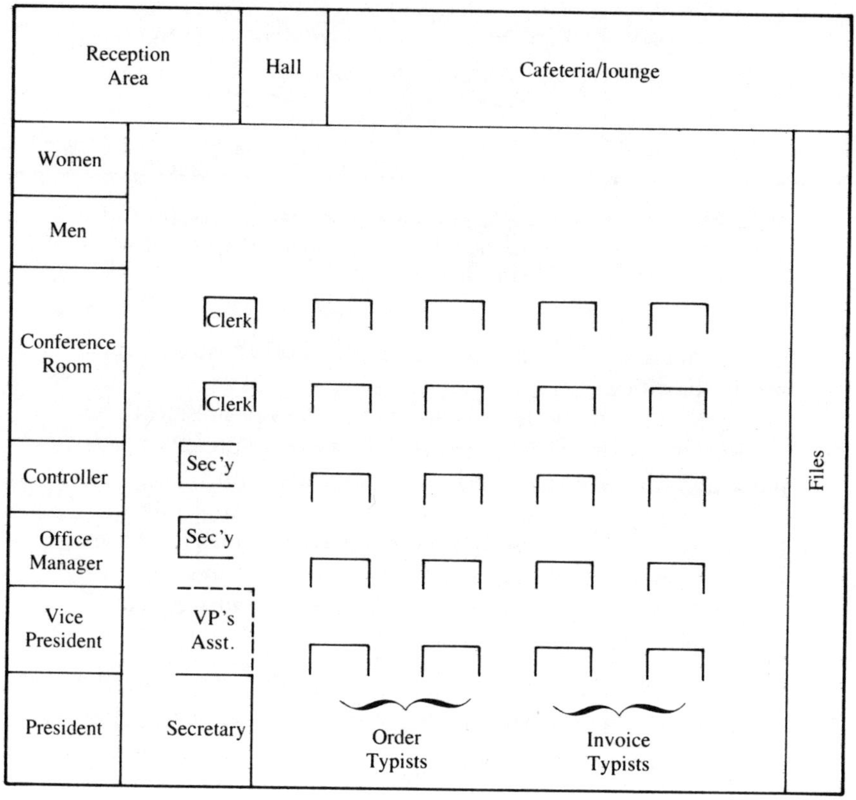

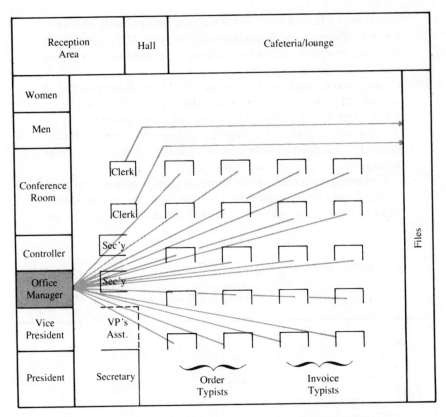

FIGURE 11. Original office layout shows that clerks and typists had to spend a good part of the day walking to and from the office manager's office and to the files.

by with doing so little work, and this affected other work attitudes within the office.

I couldn't get rid of the person—he was the vice president's administrative assistant. But I was able to rearrange the office to remove him from the main work scene [see Figure 10].

I recommended to our vice president that a semiprivate space be created to give his assistant more privacy in which to concentrate. The assistant loved this and considered it an advantage. The rest of the staff realized why it had been done and were able to devote more attention to their work.

Office layout should be evaluated for efficiency as well as personalities. Using an office map, draw arrows showing where each individual must regularly move to complete his or her work (see

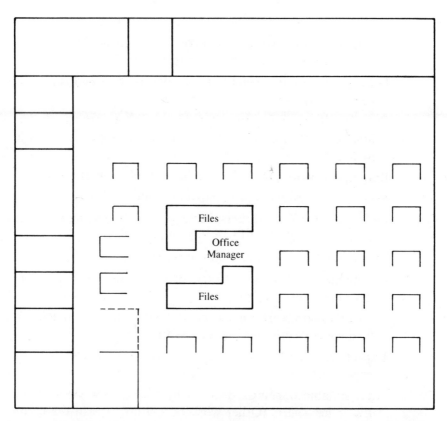

FIGURE 12. With the office manager and the files in a central location, typists and clerks were able to spend more of their time actually getting their jobs completed.

Figure 11). Then, try to rearrange the office space to cut down the number of steps (and time) used by each worker (see Figure 12).

Your own attitudes, even more than geographical relationships in the office, will affect how competent workers perform. The way you treat competent people who work for you will greatly influence what they will do. One supervisor in a large clerical office provided the following tips for working with office employees:

Remember to put yourself in their place regularly, and treat them as you would want to be treated.

Don't talk down to office workers.

Don't use them to do unnecessary or personal errands.

Encourage office workers to take full responsibility for jobs they can handle without your supervision.

Let experienced, competent office workers train and supervise new employees whenever this is possible.

Occasionally pitch in yourself and help with an urgent job that no-one wants to do, such as stuffing envelopes for a large mailing.

Praise good work regularly, and in front of co-workers.

Make any necessary reprimands in private.

Be friendly with all workers, but avoid close personal relationships that could lead to charges of favoritism.

Encourage office workers to improve their skills.

Encourage office workers to try for promotions when you believe they can handle the job.

Let workers do work their own way, not yours, if the job can be done correctly in equal or less time.

Expect only the best work, and let your staff know that you expect it.

After suitable warnings, dismiss any worker who does not do his or her share. (Other workers will only resent doing another person's work.)

INCENTIVE PLANS

Is it possible to use an incentive plan to motivate office workers? Yes, reported a number of managers interviewed.

Money incentives were the most difficult plans to establish, yet several managers had installed them in offices with work that is fairly easy to measure, such as invoice and order typing, typing pools, and word processing centers. Generally, a base number of pages, invoices, orders, and so on were set as a quota, and the typist was paid a bonus for each additional page, ten pages, or so on.

"With current estimates that a business letter now costs $3.50 or more to type and mail, it only makes sense to give a small bonus to speed up the work and cut costs," reported one office manager.

"Bonuses were fairly easy to establish for our manuscript typists," reported another manager. "A base of four error-free double-spaced pages per hour is used. If output exceeds four error-free pages, the typist receives a bonus of $0.10 per page. If error-free pages exceed six pages per hour, the bonus is paid at the rate of $0.20 per page for *all* pages. If error-free pages are produced at eight or more per hour, the typist is paid a bonus of $0.30 per page for *all* pages. It's a fair system—all of the typists we hire *can* type rapidly, but this rewards those who keep at it and really turn out the work."

"Set the base figure just a bit below what the average worker produces," suggested a supervisor who established an incentive plan for invoice typists. "Then set up increasing bonuses for additional work."

In offices where work volume was hard to measure as accurately as outlined, nonmonetary incentive systems were most often used. "Lateness and absenteeism were big problems," said one insurance company office manager. "We tried flextime, but it was very difficult to keep track of everyone's hours.

"Then we devised a time-off incentive plan. Workers accumulate extra time off for attendance and promptness. Attendance bonuses are given at the rate of five minutes for each day and five minutes for being at work on time. Essentially, this gives the worker who is always present and always on time one day off about each two months."

In another office, the supervisor assigns work deadlines and points that can be earned when a project is completed on time. When 200 points are accumulated, the worker is entitled to a free day.

"This same system could be used as a money incentive program," said the supervisor. "Each point might be worth $0.10, for example."

KEEP YOUR SENSE OF HUMOR

One of the simplest yet most effective ways to motivate office workers is using a sense of humor, reported several managers interviewed. Said one executive,

Office work is mostly dull, and if the office worker can sometimes chuckle, it relieves the monotony.

I first realized this when I had to give my secretary a rather

large number of what were essentially form letters, yet that required several variable fill-ins that only a sharp-minded person
could remember to add.

The people receiving the letters had provided both me and my
secretary with many problems in the past, and as I wrote out the
rough draft for the sample letter, I began, "Dear (Jerko)," knowing that my secretary would substitute the individual's real name
for the material in the parentheses.

"When my secretary began the letters, she really cracked up at
that salutation. And as she worked her way through the terribly
dull stack of letters, she laughed several times—probably thinking
how accurate a name it was for at least some of the people receiving the letter.

It was such a little thing, and really not very nice, I suppose.
But even today she types form letters more willingly than before—and never fails to refer to them as my "Dear Jerko letters."

Another manager stressed that humor helps unite the office
staff and that it ensures that employees will work better as a
team. "One of our staff is an excellent photographer," he said,
"and he started taking candid shots of the staff and posting them
on the bulletin board. Somewhere along the way, someone wrote
a funny caption for one of the photos. Now, it's a tradition. Everyone takes part. It relieves the monotony and we all go back
to our desks ready to work a little bit harder."

EXPLAIN WORK'S IMPORTANCE

More and better work will be forthcoming from competent office
employees if you take the trouble to explain the importance of
what they are doing, reported some managers.

"If you give some dictation to a good typist, you'll probably
get it back in a reasonable time," said one executive. "But if you
explain that the letters are the beginning of a new sales campaign
to big potential clients and that it will help to make sales if the
letters look extra sharp, you'll be pleasantly surprised how much
better the work will be.

"By explaining the importance of a project, you make the office worker a part of that project, and create a work challenge
that a competent employee will enjoy meeting.

"But," this executive warns, "don't try to tell the competent office worker that interoffice memos deserve this kind of extra care. They'll know better, and you'll negate the whole motivating effect when you *do* have important work.

"It's important that an office worker understand the whole sequence of the company's work," said a publisher. "Our business depends on advertising sales, yet office workers are mainly connected with clerical work for editorial production. Unless they know why advertising is important—that it pays their salaries—then calls from, and letters to, advertisers and prospects don't get the attention they deserve."

"Be sure office workers know what has top priority," advised a West Coast manufacturer. "Order processing and invoicing are the most important in our offices, because our income depends on these. Our office staff is regularly reminded that these come first; filing, checking phone bills, or sorting sales literature can be done when there's extra time."

One office manager in a large retailing firm holds monthly meetings of office staff to air gripes, pass along information about new projects, and to ensure that the staff is well informed about company projects and goals.

THE TITLE GAME

Don't be afraid to use titles to reward office workers. Like all of us, they enjoy having a title that carries some prestige. If they're competent office workers, titles as rewards may become even more important to them than more money.

"I learned how to play the title game when I worked in Europe for a few years," said an international sales manager. "If your title doesn't include the word 'director' there, you're nothing. Salesmen are sales directors, sales managers become chief sales directors, and so on.

"For office workers, good title words are *associate* and *assistant.*"

In one large retailing firm we surveyed, all employees are called *associates*—even the entry-level clerk-typists.

How can you change your office titles to more status-filled, motivating ones? "A typist can become an associate word processor, an invoice clerk can become an invoice associate, a gal or guy friday can be called an administrative assistant or associate, and if you have your own secretary, call him or her an executive assistant," one manager advised.

Will this use of titles cost you more money? "Many people would rather have a better title than more money," said one personnel manager. "I call it the Wizard of Oz syndrome. In that movie, the Cowardly Lion became brave when he was given a badge that said 'courage' on it. In the same way, office workers feel better about themselves when they have important-sounding titles."

"Creating new titles can be a way to get deserved raises for competent office workers when you're fighting corporate policy," recommended a manager who works in one of the largest U.S. companies. "If the title is not in general use in the company, you as the manager will probably be involved in deciding on what grade classification the job and title should be. It's a very effective way to raise employees a grade or two when they deserve it."

CHAPTER TEN

Competition serves as a good motivator.

PROFITING FROM COMPETENT MANAGERIAL WORKERS

Finding and motivating competent lower- and middle-management employees is as difficult as locating and profitably using any other type of worker. In some cases, it is more difficult, said top executives interviewed.

"My middle-management staff consists mainly of young people who are anxious to climb the career ladder and of older workers who have pretty much given up any hope of advancement," reported one company president. "That means that almost none of them are pleased with their present position and it makes motivation both essential and very difficult."

MONEY AND ITS ROLE IN MOTIVATION

While survey results show that competent workers are not as concerned with money as are less competent workers, comments from survey respondents made it clear that this is true *only* when the individual is being paid at average levels or better.

"Money alone cannot motivate most managers," said another executive, "but if a manager finds that he or she is being paid less than his or her counterpart either inside or outside the company, the demoralizing effect can be really serious."

Incentive systems, including profit-sharing plans, can help motivate managers *if* these can be tied to individual or departmental
performance.

"Our profit-sharing plan is rather meaningless so far as motivating supervisors," said a department head. "It's really just a
glorified savings plan. We put our money into the plan, and the
corporation (one of the world's largest) adds a percentage of
what we save, depending on corporate profits for the year. If my
department makes a big profit and the corporation as a whole
does badly, I get no more than the poor managers who were responsible for the weak corporate performance."

"Our plan is tied to departmental performance, with bonuses
paid according to department rather than corporate profits," said
another manager. "That provides a real incentive when you
know that what will be put into your share of the plan depends
directly on your department's bottom line."

"Salary structures only motivate you to change jobs," said a
young manager. "Big raises almost never happen once you're inside a company. Your big jumps come when you change jobs."

"That's the sort of thing a top executive should prevent," replied a large company's chief executive officer. "You spend too
much breaking in new managers. It's better to take care of them
financially."

"Perks are what I want," a young Swedish manager said. "My
tax bracket is so high even at $30,000 a year that a raise means
nothing to me—the government takes it all. But a company car,
company-subsidized mortgages—these are things that motivate
me financially."

"Stock options aren't a good motivator with the new tax
laws," reported one U. S. executive. "If I exercise an option at
a lower price than the current market value, the full-value tax
renders the value of the option literally meaningless."

STATUS AND ITS ROLE IN MOTIVATION

Status can serve as an effective motivator for many managers. Titles, prime office locations, and so on are often very important
to the younger, aggressive manager in the process of climbing
higher in the management hierarchy. In what has already been
called the Wizard of Oz syndrome, the manager who is given a

title or office that represents an improvement in status often *becomes* what he or she believes is required by that position. "There's nothing more enjoyable than promoting young, eager managers and watching them quickly develop into what their titles say they are," said one top executive.

In foreign-based subsidiaries or operations, status may be more than an ego booster for the manager. It may be essential to doing business.

"The salesperson without 'director' somewhere in his or her title can forget doing much business overseas," reported one U. S. exporter. "Without such a title, the individual is considered unimportant and is virtually ignored. So you'd better add the word manager to titles of salespeople.

The trend in the United States is in much this same direction. Key words used in titles were listed by a number of chief executive officers interviewed. These words included

director,

manager,

associate, and

officer.

"In a way, it's like learning German," said one wholesale firm's president. "You just keep adding important sounding words together to come up with the most status-filled title possible." Thus, a salesperson may become a district manager; sales director, Eastern United States; sales director, Africa; and so on. An office manager may become chief of operations, office director, and so on.

What purpose does coining such titles serve? Often, status-filled titles motivate younger and middle-level managers. In many cases, titles can substitute for a larger raise (which the company's budget or government wage controls rule out), and thus help retain a competent manager who might otherwise leave.

How do you come up with the right title to be sure it *does* motivate? "I sit down with the individual," said one company president. "I ask what he or she hopes to accomplish for the firm within the next two years. If necessary, we have a second meeting to provide time to think about it. Then, I ask them to write two or three titles they believe would be appropriate to go along with that work. Once that's done, I choose the most impressive sounding title of the lot and make that the individual's new title."

COMPETITION AS A MANAGEMENT MOTIVATOR

Competition exists within every management hierarchy, yet too seldom does the executive *use* it to motivate managers. On the contrary, when competition and its inevitable political implications are allowed to move undirected (as happens in many firms), competition can destroy management motivation, and often does.

The positive use of competition is most likely when managerial performance can be measured and compared openly, according to the executives interviewed. For example, international sales managers with various territories can have their performances compared by measuring percentages of territory sales quotas reached. Sales dollars figures would not be as meaningful a comparison or as effective a competition-related motivator, since a specific territory might not have the same current sales potential as all other territories.

Good-sized prizes, such as large bonuses, trips, and so on, can be used to add spice and motivation to competitions among managers. One Midwest factory gives a $1,000 bonus to the foreman with the greatest percentage of increase over his or her production quota.

Competition is intensified when the managers to be motivated *know* their immediate boss *and* when the top brass see reports regularly announcing competition results. "We accomplish this goal by clearly carbon copying the president and the chairman of the board on all reports," said one manager. We send competition reports to lower- or middle-level managers at home," reported another executive. "If the spouse or live-in sees it and wants the manager to beat her or his co-managers, motivation climbs." Another executive reported that he sends telegrams to the spouse of a manager who does well in competitions, congratulating the spouse on his or her supportive actions that helped the manager win.

It is possible to set up managerial competitions in almost any type of business. Begin by establishing measurable units of achievement, whether these are dollar volume of sales, units of goods manufactured, pages of material processed, and so on. Looking at current managerial performance in both average and individual output, set goals for each manager. These goals will become 100%, so that to exceed them gives one the ego lift of passing the top.

Next, establish the competition by announcing a contest with a prize, with the contest to be held over a specific period of time. Or set rewards (bonus, time off, prizes) each time the manager passes his or her monthly (weekly, quarterly) goal.

DISCIPLINE AS A MANAGEMENT MOTIVATOR

Can discipline still be used to motivate managers? Yes and no, came the replies to interview questions.

Discipline no longer has much effect in getting more work from a manager when it is used directly. That is, today's manager does not respond well to long lectures about doing better, to having his or her secretary taken away as "punishment," or to other punitive measures.

These measures may, in fact, affect his or her performance adversely and may only be of some help when he or she leaves and is working on a new job.

Firing managers is the ultimate punitive measure to control them, and it is probably not used often enough. "Sometimes you do a manager a favor by firing him or her," one executive said. "These people may really work to correct faults in the next positions they hold. Just as important, firing a manager who doesn't measure up helps motivate other managers. They get the message that you won't tolerate incompetence."

CHAPTER ELEVEN

PROFITING FROM COMPETENT PROFESSIONAL WORKERS

Many people assume that it is not necessary to motivate professional workers since they "should be" dedicated to their profession. Although professionals are usually very interested in their work, it is definitely possible to improve performance with a good motivational plan, said executives interviewed.

MONEY: THE MOST OBVIOUS MOTIVATOR

Money is the most obvious motivator for professional workers, who include engineers, staff psychologists and doctors, nurses, teachers, artists, musicians, lawyers, journalists, and so on. A look at the list of workers considered professionals, however, shows that there is a wide disparity in money each can expect to earn. Doctors, psychologists, and lawyers—even when working for a company—expect to, and do, earn very large salaries. Teachers, company artists, and others may earn a reasonable wage, but their salaries cannot be compared to those in the first group. Each of the two groups should thus be approached with separate planning when establishing a money-based motivational plan.

The Highly-Paid Professionals. Lawyers, doctors, psychologists, and others who are paid very well should be motivated by money much as you would motivate top management in any business, even if they are not partners (in a law firm, for example) or department chiefs (in hospitals, for instance). "We have a top-quality profit-sharing plan," said the head of one large law firm. "Partners receive the largest share, but associates do all right, too."

Psychologists and doctors working in private clinics usually benefit from profit-sharing plans, as well as from larger salaries than those paid by public institutions. Hospitals, public or private, can motivate top-quality personnel by backing them in applications for government or private research grants that will provide funds.

The Lower-Paid Group. Other professionals—including teachers, nurses, artists, journalists, musicians, and so on—are probably easier to motivate with money simply because their salaries are not so great.

"Money *has* to turn me on at this point," said one college professor. "I make less working for a state university than I would have had I stayed on as head of a junior high school department. And I wouldn't have had to spend money to earn a doctor's degree, either."

The sad-but-true fact is that few, if any, government institutions have funds to use for motivational programs in the traditional sense. "We do use our research funds, workshop money, and summer school funds to motivate," said one department head. "A teacher has to submit an outline of the year's accomplishments and his or her plans for the program, and decisions are held on that basis rather than on the political grounds used by many schools."

Nurses in private clinics may be included in profit-participation programs, although we found no instance of their receiving stock options or other money motivators received by doctors in the same clinics. "In our plan," said one clinic administrator, "the employee contributes a percentage of his or her salary. The clinic adds a percentage, depending on the year's profits and the level of the professional. Employees are eligible for the plan after two years of work, and become fully vested after six years of plan participation."

Company artists, journalists, and other professionals who work for private companies can be motivated with the same type of bonus and incentive plans used for managerial employees (see Chapter 10). Money can be especially important in retaining really good professionals in these areas who, without extra money for motivation, might prefer to paint portraits or write mystery novels for a living.

SECURITY AS A MOTIVATOR

Security is probably not very important to highly paid professionals, such as doctors, who can start their own practice if things become shaky in a private clinic. But security can be an extremely important motivator among lower-paid professionals. A good example is the teacher or professor who puts in many extra hours to earn tenure.

A tenure system, which basically grants employment security (except in cases of gross violation of school codes or unforeseen economic events), can be adapted to use when motivating any professional employee. Basically, granting tenure consists of an evaluation of the employee's work by both superiors and peers. In the case of a college professor, books and articles published, workshops conducted, honors won, student response, and so on are taken into consideration.

One publishing company that participated in the survey has a variation of the tenure system in operation. According to the company president

After five years, we (top management) look at an individual editor's or writer's progress. We examine volume of work, editorial honors, and quality of work. If each phase is of acceptable levels, the employee has informal tenure. I'm sure everyone knows that it takes something really drastic for us to fire anyone who passes this five-year test.

If the work is not good at this five-year level, we discuss the problems with the employee. Usually, he or she goes somewhere else.

There are similar, if not as thorough, examinations at three months, and then each year at hiring anniversary time. After each evaluation, the employee is counseled about work strengths and weaknesses. The sessions also serve as guides to giving raises. If the work is poor, no raise is given. If work is very bad, the employee will be fired.

WORK AS A MOTIVATOR

The work itself serves as the best motivator for the most competent professional employees, survey results showed. This does not mean that top management can dump a lot of work on a professional and then sit back and assume that he or she will be happy. The professional is motivated by doing the work he or she likes most and is best at doing, and will do other work as required in order to get these assignments.

For example, if a nurse is especially good with children, a wise administrator will assign him or her to work with children if at all possible. "I don't mind putting out the extra effort for the kids," said a nurse. "Somehow when adults are involved, I can't make myself do as much."

Teachers will generally teach in their area of greatest interest, but administrators can encourage young professionals in the wrong field to make a lateral switch. "I was teaching electronic engineering," said a college professor, "but my heart was still in my music minor. The head of the department persuaded me to get my doctor's degree in music—and I can't imagine what my life would be like today if I weren't teaching music. It means everything to me, and I put my whole life into it."

Journalists may be hired for one job, but moved to another beat if the work is of greater interest and has a stronger motivating effect. "I watch new faces," said a chief editor. "A young gal or guy may be hired to writer fillers, but eventually I want them working beats they love and will work their guts out for, if necessary."

COMPETITION: A NO-COST OR LOW-COST MOTIVATOR

Professionals at all pay levels are motivated by competition. A doctor may put in many extra hours to be considered the best in the field; so may a teacher or journalist.

The administrator may also like to use competition as a motivator, since it does not *have* to be tied to an incentive or other money-related plan. "Competition is sparked," said one clinic administrator, "by establishing a unit of output and making everyone's output available to everyone else. Our staff of psychologists crowd around the lounge bulletin board on Friday afternoons to see who clocked the most patient therapy hours."

One editor set up an editorial workload system comparing numbers of weight-loaded pages (with different factors depending on the difficulty of writing or editing) produced by each staff member for each publication issue. Issue reports are also combined into annual reviews, used to help determine wage increases.

CHAPTER TWELVE

PROFITING FROM COMPETENT INDUSTRIAL WORKERS

Finding competent industrial workers is difficult, and motivating them is an even greater challenge. Industrial geniuses who once spent their time on planning new ways to produce products now more and more often must find new ways to encourage workers to stick to assembly-line or other industrial jobs.

MONEY AS A MOTIVATOR OF INDUSTRIAL WORKERS

The largest number of industrial incentive plans are tied to money. From piece-rate systems (where workers are paid for each unit produced) to attendance bonuses for coming to work regularly, money is a big factor in trying to encourage the industrial worker. Some of the most successful of these plans are shown in Table 13.

The manager should be careful to build safeguards against production of goods of unacceptable quality into any money-related motivational plan used. Even competent workers will make quality-cutting moves to produce more units and make more money, unless such units are excluded from the incentive program.

TABLE 13. Money-Related Motivational Plans for Use with
Industrial Workers

Plan name	Description	Results/comments
Absenteeism control	Working conditions are improved, workers are given more responsibility, work flow is channeled more evenly, worker conflicts are resolved, good work is recognized, and supervisor–worker communication is improved to overcome problems pinpointed by a New York telephone company survey that says absences cost U.S. businesses about $10 billion per year.	Bonuses can be tied to any or all steps described to reinforce them.
Attendance bonus	A share of savings that result from regular attendance (such as 30%) is paid to employees with consistent work attendance records. Average absence rates are calculated, and bonuses are paid when actual absences are less than this amount. Variations of the plan use the same system to reward punctuality and efficiency.	Data should be programmed into computerized payroll for lowest-cost administration.
Group	Workers who produce units as a team are paid per unit of production, with payment divided in a manner giving skilled workers the greater shares.	

PSYCHOLOGICAL MOTIVATION OF INDUSTRIAL WORKERS

Managers don't need to be psychologists to motivate industrial workers, but the use of some psychological methods can help, said those interviewed. The best techniques mentioned are outlined below.

Attitude Surveys and Scales. Employees (at least 500) in large companies can be asked to take part in a survey to measure workers' attitudes toward work, the work place, supervisors, and the employing company. Replies should be kept anonymous to encourage participation, and employees should be assured that the company will take some action in areas found to be unsatisfactory by survey results.

"Just being the focal point via the survey seemed to motivate a lot of the assembly-line workers," reported one supervisor. "I guess it was the extra attention. Even if the effect wears off, it stepped up productivity for now."

Behavioral Conditioning. A number of industrial managers surveyed used behavioral conditioning to motivate workers. "Mainly it's a matter of reinforcing what they already know," said one manager. "I start by reminding workers that the company must be profitable in order for them to have jobs. Next, I use praise, promotions, and so on to *reinforce* good work. I try to keep the work place in the best order to let workers know that their mental attitudes are important to the company. Jobs are set up to be completed by teams, so that each worker has more responsibility and actually completes the manufacture of something, rather than just screwing on 500 bolts per day."

Frequency of reinforcement is important, suggested another supervisor. "Aversive reinforcement, such as reprimanding workers, is not as effective as positive reinforcement, such as praise for good work," reported one foreman.

Brainstorming. "Brainstorming works when you want to improve industrial production techniques," said one foreman interviewed, "but only if you use the workers on the line—they know what it's all about."

Workers are encouraged to imagine any possible way to improve output and to write these methods down, no matter how wild they seem. The foreman can then put the suggestions on a blackboard so that the group can discuss them.

One danger of the method is inadequate follow-through by managerial staff. "If you don't put the best ideas into action," cautioned one manager, "they can't change *anything.*"

Co-partnership. Using this technique, management motivates industrial workers by involving them in responsibility for the business's success as well as sharing in the profits.

"We give each worker as much responsibility as he or she can handle," reported one manager. "Competent workers generally like to be given more responsibility, and this helps us retain them—probably even more than the share of profits they receive."

Fatigue Study. Fatigue study is the measurement of work place and other causes of employee fatigue. "We can motivate workers greatly by correcting as many of the causes of work fatigue as possible," said one supervisor. "For example, corrections in the physical working place—such as better lighting, a comfortable working temperature, good ventilation, and correctly designed equipment—can make a great deal of difference.

"Fatigue can be reduced, and work speed and quality increased, by limiting overtime assignments and through the use of efficient scheduling and breaks."

Gestalt Techniques. One manager interviewed said he had experienced good results in motivating industrial workers using a variety of gestalt psychology techniques. These included the use of role playing to resolve arguments. "At labor union meetings, I often suggest we argue from the other's point of view for a few minutes in the middle of sessions," he said. "It helps us understand each other."

Other gestalt rules used by this manager include one that all workers and supervisors speak *directly* to each other; no third-party conversations are allowed. "If this rule is followed," he claims, "a worker can't say 'Joe' told him one thing when the supervisor says she issued a different instruction. Any instructions or other conversations are to be addressed directly to the person involved."

Supervisors are taught to ask workers *what* they are doing and *how*. "These two questions focus the employee's attention on the work, and improve output," the manager claims.

Finally, questions are not used. According to gestalt theory, these often mask inferences of blame. "A supervisor doesn't snap, 'Why don't you have that work done yet?' " reports the manager. "Instead, he or she may say, 'The work is late, so I'll help you until it's completed.' "

Hawthorne Technique. Variations of this method (splitting workers into teams) were used by a number of managers interviewed in their attempts to motivate industrial workers. *"Good* workers are bored to death by the old assembly-line procedure of making the same motion over and over all day," said one supervisor. "We split workers into teams of six. Each worker learns several jobs, and each team produces a finished product. This maintains a pride in workmanship, alleviates boredom, and generally increases total work output by more than 10%."

Hypnosis. One manager reported that his company is using an experimental hypnosis program to motivate industrial workers. Employees, who were paid piece rates with a guaranteed wage, volunteered for the program. Suggestions were made, during a deep trance state, that the worker would be able to work faster.

"For the first week after posthypnotic suggestions of this kind are made, output in a good worker will usually be up 20–40%," the manager reports. "Eventually the level works its way back to normal. We're getting increased results with the use of additional 'booster hypnotic sessions' now."

Iemoto. A Japanese manager working for an American firm reported that he has successfully used the Japanese method of Iemoto to motivate industrial workers. "Basically, Iemoto is fostering the feeling that the work group is like a family. The supervisor must assume "head of the family" responsibilities toward the workers, and they in turn will react by expecting group members to pitch in and work together to meet work goals."

Job Design. This technique was mentioned by many managers as being important in motivating industrial workers. It includes job enlargement (giving workers more duties), job enrichment (giving workers more responsibility and challenges), and job loading (offering interesting work as a reward for completing meaningless but necessary labor).

Open-Door Policy. Several managers interviewed also reported that industrial workers produce more when the "door is always open" to receive problems or gripes. "Every worker knows that he or she can bring me any real gripe or problem," said one manager. "We work together to solve the problems without a lot of red tape."

Presentation of Costs. A department head reported that his workers correct time or cost problems when he puts a dollar figure on them. "Most workers don't realize what an unacceptable unit costs when it is not manufactured correctly, for example," he said. "We constantly remind workers what each unit returned by quality control costs—in dollars and cents—and how this affects their profit sharing—also in dollars and cents. Pretty soon a new worker takes up the cry, 'Be careful, Joe, or that'll be $89.50 down the drain.' "

Prize Incentives. One manager awards workers prizes, selected from a catalog (similar to a green-stamp catalog), in return for the accumulation of points. Point values are assigned for regular attendance, promptness, increased output, or improved quality of workmanship.

Productivity Bargaining. This method is often used, according to managers interviewed, to obtain greater output from industrial workers. During labor negotiations, management gives labor some requested benefit in exchange for the use of new methods or equipment to increase productivity.

Sandwich Method. Foremen can use the method of "sandwiching" criticism between deserved work compliments to ease the task of reprimanding industrial workers. By making the workers aware of their good points, the technique also makes it easier for them to accept criticism.

Short-Interval Scheduling. In this technique the supervisor plans work units that can be completed in short intervals, such as an hour. This aids motivation, as the worker can easily see what needs to be done and by what time.

CHAPTER THIRTEEN

PROFITING FROM COMPETENT
SERVICE WORKERS

Service workers, such as waiters and waitresses, hairdressers, taxi drivers, bank tellers, and dry cleaning workers present some interesting motivational challenges. This is so because service-oriented businesses are, naturally, those that involve no product, but rather depend on service itself. This means that the personality of the employee is the key factor. The service worker should like people, should be outgoing, and should want to provide the best service possible.

Because some service workers (like waiters and hairdressers) depend on tips, while others (such as dry cleaning employees) never see a tip, motivation must be discussed in terms of both money-related and other factors.

MONEY-RELATED MOTIVATION WORKS BEST

Service workers are often paid the minimum wage, which means that monetary motivation probably has the best chance of getting results.

Waiters and waitresses generally depend in large part on tips for their living, and a good manager can do much to ensure that these employees earn the best tips possible. "We train waiters in the basics of good service," says one manager. "And we provide anonymous examples of weekly tips earned—from the lowest to the highest—to show how much more they *can* earn if they do provide top-quality service."

"It's important to back up your waitresses with a good kitchen and clean-up system," reported another manager. "She *can't* give good service if the food is badly or slowly cooked or if the busboy or -girl doesn't clean tables, fill water glasses, and so on."

"Management decisions affect where I work," a waiter said. "I won't work on a team system where my income depends on another waiter who might or might not do a good job. And I won't work where there's a system combining all tips. I do everything possible to please my customers, and I want the tips they leave."

"Kitchen help presents a problem in the matter of monetary motivation," admitted one restaurant owner. "Waiters, the head waiter, and the busboys all get a cut of the tips. The chef gets a big salary. But the salad person, the fry cook, and the dishwashers are left out. It's up to management to offer some sort of profit-sharing plan to make these important workers add more to the operation's success."

"Hotel problems are much the same as those of a restaurant," said one manager. "In a top-quality operation, tips motivate most of the staff—bellmen, waiters and waitresses, maids, and so on. Management needs to implement a profit-sharing plan to motivate the others—desk clerks, the housekeeper, handymen, and so on."

Generally, two payment systems exist for hairdressers. In one, the individual is paid a salary and also receives tips. In the other, the hairdresser receives a percentage of the income from his or her work—usually 40 or 50%—and also receives tips. Which system is best?

"The hairdresser works more carefully if he or she isn't trying to rush customers through to up the take," said one salon manager interviewed.

"The best operators will only work where they're assured a cut of the income they produce," countered another manager.

"Good operators *do* want to work where they earn a percentage of the take," said a hairdresser. "It's the fairest method."

Managers can add to hairdressers' incomes by using switch-work techniques, according to survey results. In this method, one operator shampoos a customer's hair while a second completes the haircutting or other work. Often, both will receive a tip.

PSYCHOLOGICAL MOTIVATION OF SERVICE WORKERS

There are also nonmonetary ways to motivate service workers. "The most important thing is the customer's acknowledgment of the quality of service," said a waiter who was interviewed. "That means more than any tip to me."

"Giving the wherewithal to provide good service is essential," said one bank manager. "When a branch has adequate facilities and an adequate number of tellers, the same tellers will give better service than they will when there are too few of them assigned to the job. As the customers grumble about waiting, tellers generally react by moving slower—not faster. It's psychological."

As the Metropolitan Transit Authority does in New York City, it is possible to use customer-judged awards to employees who provide good service. Bus drivers nominated by passengers are eligible for "Big Wheel" awards in this system.

Competitions can also be geared to providing winners with time off, award certificates, or both. These competitions can be based on customer appraisal, number of customers served, and so on.

"The real way to motivate many service workers," said a resort manager, "would be to educate the public to treat service workers like human beings rather than inanimate objects. If one of the big service industries would launch a consumer campaign along those lines, and if the public responded to it, the level of service would definitely improve."

CHAPTER FOURTEEN

The possibility of advancement can help keep a good worker on the job.

WHY DOES THE COMPETENT WORKER STAY ON THE JOB?

Competent workers surveyed gave a number of reasons for staying on a particular job. The chance to do work that seemed most meaningful to them, along with the chance to progress within the company (and to be fairly paid), provided the greatest motivation to stick with a job—at least for the top-rated workers.

"I believe that if I work hard enough, I could be president of the company some day," said one young employee who was interviewed. "In the meantime, I do work hard because I enjoy what I'm doing and because I want to advance."

THE SUPERVISOR–EMPLOYEE RELATIONSHIP IS IMPORTANT

How an employee views his or her supervisor is also a critical factor, according to survey results. The competent worker wants to respect his or her boss, and wants to feel that the boss both recognizes and acknowledges his or her work efforts (either in money or in status terms, and preferably in both).

"I was carrying a heavy workload and doing a good job, but my boss only seemed resentful about it," reported one office worker. "I got so frustrated that I started looking for another job on the QT. Then my boss quit! What a difference the new supervisor has made. If anything, I work harder. But the top brass knows how much I do now—my boss tells them. And he hands out praise when it's deserved, too."

"I left one job where my boss found fault with everything because I hadn't done it exactly as he would have done it," said another top-rated worker. "There was nothing wrong with the work—he admitted that. He just wanted everyone to use his old-fashioned, slower methods like figuring on paper instead of using a calculator. He kept saying, 'It's a mistake to depend on machines.' "

"Boss–worker personality clashes are the biggest reason for changing jobs, if you ask me," said a personnel department head. "Applicants don't put that as a reason on their job application forms very often. They write 'left for better job.' But sooner or later, most applicants say something that lets you know personalities were very much involved."

"It's important for the manager to realize that he or she may be the key factor as to whether good workers stay or go," said a company psychologist. "If more than 10% of a staff *quits* per year (those who are fired are a different problem), the manager should look at the real reasons for their changes. If the reason is usually one of personalities, the manager had better start treating workers as he or she would want to be treated."

JOBS SHOULD KEEP PACE WITH WORKERS' GROWTH

To keep good employees, it is essential to make sure that their jobs keep pace with their growth, reported many managers interviewed. This can be accomplished by promoting employees when suitable openings exist. If such job openings don't exist, the manager can create new jobs and titles and be sure that each worker is given *all* of the responsibility he or she can handle.

"I always want my staff to have some work which is a challenge," said one Midwestern plant superintendent. "If they have to stretch their abilities to do a job, they'll continue to grow instead of becoming complacent."

"Providing variety in work can help keep good workers from job-hopping," reported another manager. "Top-quality people are more likely to get bored doing routine work all of the time, so it's important to alternate tasks."

"Good workers should be encouraged to learn new skills," said the head of an exporting company. "It makes the company a more versatile one."

"You have to be willing to tell a good worker if it's time for him or her to move on," said one manager. "In our company, top management is limited to family, since it's a family-owned business. When a young manager reaches a certain point, I tell him or her that I like their work but that they're capable of more. Often, I help them find a spot. And many times, the employees' new companies end up doing business with ours."

DOES MONEY HOLD COMPETENT WORKERS?

According to survey results and interviews, a *lack* of adequate salary will help you lose good workers, but money is not the most important factor in retaining top-rated employees. In fact, money was more important to the less competent worker, survey results show.

In Britain, an excess of benefits or "perks" can actually cut the quality of a manager's work, according to a recent report from the London *Financial Times.* Those in middle-level management usually receive such perks as a company car, their children's school fees, furniture, and, in some cases clothing for business wear. These perks are provided in an attempt to give remuneration that can't be eaten away by high levels of taxation. With these benefits, managers become so dependent on the company, the report states, that they become less aggressive and more anxious to maintain a low profile—and, thus, their benefits.

"It is important to know the industry average for payment for a position, and to see that a really good worker is paid more than this figure," advised one company president. "Then stop worrying about it (once you're paying more than the average)—more money than that won't help you hold the person."

Money is most likely to be helpful in retaining good industrial workers. "There's not much else to motivate a bright, competent assembly-line worker," reported one supervisor. "He or she is definitely doing the job to earn the most money possible. Maybe there are older parents to be supported or whatever, but money's the motivator here."

Service workers are more likely to be motivated by money, too.

"Sure I take the big tippers myself," said the senior stylist of a hairdressing salon. "I've been putting up with all kinds of people and their complaints for 20 years. I'm entitled."

DON'T FORGET THE WORKERS' FAMILIES

According to survey results, families or love partners are the one element of the most competent workers' lives that are more important to them than their work. For this reason, a manager can often retain good workers by keeping their families or love partners in mind. The problem with this fact is that not every good worker wants his or her family considered in the same way.

"Some of my workers like it when we hold Christmas parties that include their families; others resent it," complained one manager. "It's hard to know exactly what to do in regard to families to please everyone."

For a start, be sure that your benefits program provides good coverage for families, recommended a number of managers in major companies. "We're providing insurance coverage for live-in partners whether the employee is married or not," reported one manager, "so long as the couple has lived together long enough to meet common-law marriage rulings in our state. It costs the company more, but we believe it's worth it."

Other companies offer a smorgasboard of compensation, with several benefits available. For example, one large firm offers hospitalization, major medical, dental, disability, and life insurance coverage. The employee may choose three of these for the whole family at no cost, and can also have one or both of the remaining two benefits by paying a small monthly fee.

"A married person with a family to support usually will want all five benefits," said the head of the firm's personnel department. "A single person may not care about the disability or life insurance."

Most good employees appreciate managerial recognition of their family's role in their ability to work well. "My boss sends a telegram to my husband thanking him for his support when I win a sales contest," said one saleswoman. "He sends flowers to the guys' wives when they win. It's a nice gesture and it lets our families know the boss realizes how many hours we spend away from them when we're on the road."

Managers interviewed say that they generally try to be interested in the good worker's family when he or she wants to talk about them, but that it is important not to give advice in regard to the personal problems that inevitably arise. "Even when workers ask for advice," said one manager, "they may resent it later if things don't turn out as desired."

Company picnics and after-hours parties that include families can create more problems than they're worth, reported several of the managers interviewed.

"The last company picnic we had resulted in too much intoxication and too many jealous husbands and wives," reported a company president. "I decided right then that we'd forget the large-scale socializing and keep our relationships to business ones in the future."

"The good manager should realize that it is natural for families or love partners to come first—even with the best workers," said another company head. "A good worker can put the firm first *occasionally,* when it's really necessary. But the manager should be sure it *is* necessary before asking that of the worker."

CHAPTER FIFTEEN

COMPETENCE MAY NOT LAST FOREVER

One of the saddest experiences for a business manager is to take over a new department and find it filled with workers who were once competent, but who now are not. Even worse, perhaps, is to watch the quality of an individual's work deterioriate under your direct supervision. But it is a fact: Just because a worker is competent when he or she is hired does not guarantee that such competence will last forever.

Can the deterioration process be stopped or reversed? And if it cannot, what can or should be done with the once-competent worker?

WHAT CAUSES A LOSS OF COMPETENCE?

There are many factors that can cause a deterioration of competence in a once-good worker. Many are related to poor managerial practices; others are not.

Management-Related Causes. Results of a study conducted by Wagner–Hohns–Inglis, Inc., a consulting firm, recently showed that most causes of competence loss among construction workers can be related to management's failure to provide workers with the four things they need to do their jobs: materials, instruction, equipment, or recognition. Many managers we interviewed said that this same failure extends to nearly all industries and that it causes a decline in worker competence at all levels.

"I was really putting the pressure on a salesman last week," said one district sales manager. "He's been way under quota this year, even though he used to be a damn good salesman.

"Anyway, he let me blow off steam for awhile. Then he said, 'Fred, I've had more than my share of *orders*, but the factory's behind schedule. I can't sell what hasn't been produced. Besides, my customers are very tired of promised delivery dates that aren't met.'

"I felt pretty silly after that because he was right. He can't sell anything if we don't provide the goods to be sold. I'm turning the pressure the other way now, on my bosses, to get the merchandise produced."

The lack of necessary materials is a particularly common cause of what seems to be decreased competence—but is actually decreased productivity—in assembly-line work. "When I see workers sitting around, I've learned to make sure they have the parts or other needed materials *before* I start yelling," said a foreman in an automobile assembly plant.

Instruction is another necessary element for any worker to do his or her job competently. "We switched to a new computerized system," reported one office manager. "Of course, we instructed workers in how to use the system. Even so, we began to notice a slowdown among older workers who had been fast under the old system, while the younger workers did better with the new system. There were a lot of discussions, with recommendations for everything from using two systems to getting rid of everyone over 35.

"I decided to start asking questions. It turned out that most of the younger workers had used the computerized system or one similar to it when training in college. The older workers hadn't ever seen a similar system. Of course, the older workers *should* have said, 'We don't understand—teach us better.' But I guess they were too intimidated by the new system and the fact that the younger people *did* understand how to use it."

Computerized and other modern equipment, as well as the lack of suitable equipment, can appear to decrease a worker's competence. "Sam used to turn in his share of stories," said a newspaper editor, "But in the last few years, I noticed his byline coming across my desk less and less often. On assigned stories, he was always late, it seemed.

"Finally, when one story came in several days late, I stopped by his desk rather than call him in. He was working on a story and the sound of his manual Royal typewriter was obvious—too obvious.

"All around him, reporters were typing stories on silent electric typewriters that were hooked into an electronic editing system. "Sam had talked the copy chief into having a typist keyboard his stories into the system and provide a printout for him to proofread. Then the typist had to keyboard the corrections. What should have taken one step was being done in four operations. No wonder the others on the staff turned in more work!"

"Is that management's fault?" we asked the editor.

"Sure," he replied. "Part of keeping your good workers competent is making sure they have new, improved equipment and that they know how to use it—and then, that they do use it."

Lack of recognition is a common cause of the decline of worker competence, although it is the worker's problem as well as management's, according to those interviewed. "Every worker needs praise from his or her boss to encourage top-level work," said one manager. "The manager who doesn't use praise and recognition as motivational tools is asking for real trouble.

"By the same token, the worker who does good work but never is recognized is at fault, too. He or she should find a job where recognition *is* available."

Other Causes. Sometimes once-competent workers become incompetent for reasons that have nothing whatsoever to do with management policies. These cases are more difficult, executives say, because they cannot be corrected by a simple change in policy.

"Age is one factor," reported an East Coast manager. "There may be plenty of competent 70-year-olds working, but our company is laced with 55-year-olds who are mentally and physically tired. They're 20-year employees and no-one wants to fire them, yet they're paid more than their work is worth."

Poor health, at this or any age, can also be a cause of lower competence levels, and this is the reason that some companies require annual physical examinations for all or some of their workers.

"Personal problems can lead to a temporary—or permanent—reduction in competence," said an office manager. "You can never know how a death or a serious illness in a family, or a divorce, will affect a worker. Some will work harder than ever; some come to a halt as far as productivity is concerned."

RECOGNIZING INCOMPETENCE
IN ONCE-COMPETENT WORKERS

If the manager is to try to halt the beginnings of incompetence in a good worker, he or she needs to recognize the danger signs. A list of 12 key warning signs was assembled from interviews with top executives in all industries. If an individual shows several of these danger signs, the executives warn, it is especially important to take action quickly:

1. Less work completed than previously.
2. Less work completed than by the average worker.
3. Work often completed long after deadlines have passed.
4. Poor attendance and punctuality.
5. Frequent talk about "the old days" or "the way it was."
6. Frequent references to co-workers who left the company some years ago.
7. Frequent complaints about new workers and failure to accept them as equals.
8. Reluctance to use new methods or equipment.
9. Desire that subordinates work only his or her way.
10. Frequent inaccuracy in work details.
11. Frequent lies about work completed or covering up of work problems.
12. Inappropriate behavior with customers, management, or co-workers.

Less Work. Unless individual productivity records are maintained, it may be difficult to measure the worker's output against his or her own past level of productivity. Regular productivity assessments are recommended by some managers to solve this problem. "We use both quarterly and annual output reports," one manager said. "A serious dip in productivity levels can signal company as well as individual work problems."

This sort of assessment also helps the manager measure the worker's output against that of the average employee. "If a top producer slows down as he or she ages," said one executive, "but still is above average, we have to accept the slower pace and be grateful to have a good worker."

Late Work. Completing work after the deadline date can also indicate a slowing down. Or it can mean that the worker has lost interest in his or her job. "Sometimes late work means mismanagement," cautioned an executive. "It could mean deadlines that are unreasonable, a lack of needed equipment or instruction, or many other factors that are the manager's not the worker's fault."

Poor Attendance, Punctuality. Managers agree that increased absence or tardiness, many long lunch hours, and leaving early frequently are all signs of less work interest. "I look at our operations first when an employee's attendance pattern changes," reported an office manager. "Generally, workers avoid work when they're unhappy—with the work, their boss, or whatever."

Old Days and Old Ways. Perhaps the most important danger signs are when an employee talks continually about the old days and about co-workers long gone, and refuses to even try new methods or equipment. If in a managerial position, the employee may try to force subordinates to use his or her (old, naturally) methods.

"I call this danger sign the 'Looking at a Dead Horse Syndrome,'" chuckled a 68-year-old manager (who belies the thought that age affects competence). "No matter what their ages or how good they were once, workers who start on this 'old days' stuff are on the road to incompetence."

"Refusal to accept young or new workers, especially women or minorities who were 'never in power before,' is also a danger sign that can mean incompetence is taking root," reported a company president.

"Managers who can't accept variations in traditional business roles are also sending up danger signs," said a company vice president. "I mean those who are uncomfortable with male secretaries, gay managers, black professionals, and so on."

Poor Work. Inaccurate work can provide new costs for the company, as well as serving as a danger sign of the increasing incompetence of a once-competent worker. "One of our people has increased her error factor about 120% this year," the head of a brokerage firm reported. "Her last miscalculation cost us nearly $78,000—and that's too much incompetence for me."

Lying. As an employee's competence level slips, he or she may realize it and try to cover up the telltale facts. "My top salesman fell apart this year," reported one sales manager. "But instead of talking the problem over with me, he kept turning in this long list of call reports. I couldn't understand why his sales weren't up.

"Then I saw one of his customers at a convention. 'Where's Joe been?' he asked. 'I haven't seen him in months!' This guy's name had been on several of Joe's call reports."

Inappropriate Behavior. Workers who change the way they behave—especially with customers—are showing clear danger signs of growing incompetence, managers say. "We recently had lunch with a German customer," said the head of an export firm. "To my horror, the salesman began talking about World War II halfway through the meal. The customer clammed up, and I changed the subject, but we haven't had any orders since.

"Even a year ago, that salesman would have known better than to bring up such a subject—he was really sharp. It's my fault, too, for not realizing what had happened to him."

DEALING WITH LOSS OF COMPETENCE

As mentioned above, it is simplest to deal with loss of worker competence that stems from poor management policies. Assuming that someone in management spots the policy or policies to blame, rather than blaming the workers, policy changes can solve the problems simply.

In the case of the newspaper reporter already mentioned, for example, the chief editor had all reporters trained to the necessary level of skill to use the new electronic editing system. Old-fashioned equipment was sold so that no-one would be tempted to use it because it was more familiar and, thus, more comfortable.

Dealing with competence loss resulting from nonmanagement causes, however, is more difficult. "With a group of apathetic managers in their fifties, I begin by trying new motivational techniques," reported a management consultant. "If that doesn't work, I put them all on warning. And if that doesn't work, I begin to dismiss them one by one.

"Usually one dismissal is enough. They've believed they couldn't be fired, and when it happens to even one of their group, a lot of them really wake up for the first time in years.

"Some will be resentful and will find new jobs—which is perfectly okay if they aren't producing much anyway. It's better to get rid of them at 55. At 65, the company is more apt to be liable for an age-discrimination suit.

"I recommend this exact procedure to managers who have inherited a department full of nonproducers."

"When an older worker's incompetence is really just a matter of his or her being tired of it all, I encourage early retirement," said the president of one large firm. "Depending on years of service and just how incompetent the person is, we may offer even earlier than usual retirement—at 58, say."

Personal problems are probably the most difficult causes of incompetence a manager faces. The difficulty lies in the fact that most managers train themselves to keep out of their subordinates' personal problems and lives.

"I can overlook a decline in good work caused by a death, illness, or a divorce if it doesn't go on *too* long," one manager said. "If the decline lasts longer than a few weeks, some action has to be taken.

"I usually talk to the employee and suggest professional help if that seems indicated. I try to reason with rather than threaten the employee. "If the worker doesn't improve and takes no steps to get help, I have to issue a warning.

"If that doesn't help, the next step is to dismiss the worker. Sometimes that wakes him or her up to perform well on the next job."

IF INCOMPETENCE PERSISTS, WHAT DO YOU
OWE THE WORKER?

What about the good worker who has become incompetent and who cannot be motivated to work well again? If you have genuinely tried to work out the problems and have failed, most managers—and the author—say that dismissal or early retirement (when appropriate) are the only possible alternatives.

"You're calling this book *The Competence Game*," one manager summed up, "and finding and using good workers is like a very difficult, challenging game, I guess. Yet business is not a game; it depends on good workers. And we can't afford to keep anyone who is not competent."

INDEX